SIGNS AND MEANINGS

SIGNS AND MEANINGS

World and Text
in Ancient Christianity

R. A. MARKUS

LIVERPOOL UNIVERSITY PRESS

First published 1996 by
LIVERPOOL UNIVERSITY PRESS
Senate House, Abercromby Square, Liverpool, L69 3BX

British Library Cataloguing-in-Publication Data
A British Library CIP Record is available
ISBN 0–85323–721–2 *cased*
0–85323–731–X *paper*

Text set in Linotron 202 Garamond by
Wilmaset Limited, Birkenhead, Wirral
Printed and bound in the European Union by
The Alden Press in the City of Oxford

For Dorothy Emmet

Contents

PREFACE

The occasion for this book was furnished by the invitation to give the Forwood Lectures in the University of Liverpool. The dedication to Dorothy Emmet signals the huge debt of gratitude I owe to a distinguished philosopher, the best of teachers and a faithful friend. In dedicating the volume to her I am conscious that these lectures fail to meet the standards of rigour and the clarity she would have wanted to encourage. I well know that there are obscurities, both in detail and, what is worse, in my overall argument. I publish them here notwithstanding my failure to achieve the clarity I have regretfully forsworn, in the belief that there is an important theme not so far recognised and in the hope that others may be able to clarify and elaborate what I have left obscure.

I want to place on record here the debt I owe to several friends for generous help with criticism and suggestions: Lewis Ayres, Kate Cooper, Conrad Leyser and Anthony Thiselton. I have adopted many of their suggestions; my failure to adopt more of them reflects my obstinacy rather than their generosity or critical acumen.

Chapters 1 and 2 correspond to the two lectures given in November 1995. I have not altered the substance of the lectures as given and retained the occasionally conversational style. I have, however, included the parts of the lectures which the time-limits compelled me to omit from them as delivered. Nicholas Wolterstorff's book, *Divine discourse. Philosophical reflections on the claim that God speaks* (Cambridge, 1995) had been published only very shortly before the lectures were given; I was unable to take it into account.

Chapters 3, 4 and 5 are papers previously published on subjects related to the theme of the lectures. Chapter 3, 'Augustine on signs', is not, as I thought when I wrote it, in the mid-1950s, quite the first study of its subject. I was not then aware of the book by K. Kuypers, *Der Zeichen- und Wortbegriff im Denken Augustins* (Amsterdam, 1934). My paper still seems, however, to have opened a long series of studies on its subject, and is still frequently referred to. It has been justly criticised by a number of subsequent writers, especially by Darrell Jackson (references given in Chapter 4, notes 3 and 7); I have made the required changes in Chapter 4. Of recent work on Stoic logic the most important is Catherine Atherton's *Stoics on ambiguity* (Cambridge, 1993). Although it has quite transformed our knowledge of Stoic logic, so far as I can tell, it has not undermined what I wrote of Augustine's theory of signs and its relation to Stoic logic. My central evaluation of Augustine's originality still seems valid.[1] I have retained here the Appendix to the original paper, on the terminology I used in it. The authors and the works referred to there are not those one would choose today to clarify the terminology; but the note is still, I think, useful to clarify what was said then. Two books, G. P. O'Daly, *Augustine's philosophy of mind* (London, 1987) and J. M. Rist, *Augustine. Ancient thought baptized* (Cambridge, 1994) contain important discussions of the subject matter of this paper. I have noted relevant qualifications in Chapter 4, and in the notes to that chapter. I have not been able to read Karla Pollmann, *Doctrina Christiana. Untersuchungen zu den Anfängen der christlichen Hermeneutik von Augustinus, De doctrina Christiana* (Habilitationsschrift. Konstanz, 1995) in time to take account of it here.

In Chapter 4 I return to the theme of Augustine on signs, especially in the *De doctrina Christiana* as that work now appears in the context of more recent interests and more recent

---

1 I must plead guilty to her charge (p. 294 note 69) that in my article (reprinted here as Chapter 3) I do not 'always do full justice to the work's [*de Magistro*] subtlety or its dialectical nature'. Her discussion of Augustine's argument here is on pp. 294–98. As it is not immediately relevant to the purpose in hand, I do not here summarise it.

work on the subject of signs. I refrained in this study from trying to provide a more up-to-date attempt to correlate Augustine's vocabulary with that of modern writers, especially De Saussure's, in the belief that no useful equivalence can be established. In this study I touch here (and more fully in Chapter 1) on the importance Augustine – like many modern writers – attached to the notion that meaning has meaning only in communities: linguistic, textual and interpretative communities, constituted by shared traditions of speaking, reading and interpreting.

The example I took of such a shared tradition of meaning, in Chapter 5, that of the demons enlisted in the exercise of magic, is one in which Augustine made both a distinctive contribution to ancient theories, and one which is a powerful application of his general theory of signs and thus throws much light on it.

In my account of Augustine's use of the Pauline text 'The letter killeth, but the Spirit giveth life' (2 Cor. 3:6) on page 13, I failed to note that although in his later writings Augustine preferred to see the verse as bearing a different meaning, he still defended the legitimacy of the interpretation he had given it in his early works. This lessens, though it does not eliminate, the contrast between his and Gregory's use of the verse.

Chapter 3 was originally published in *Phronesis* 2 (1957), and is reprinted with the permission of Van Gorcum & Co.; Chapter 4 was published in *De doctrina Christiana: A classic of Western culture*, ed. D. W. H. Arnold & P. Bright (Christianity and Judaism in Antiquity, vol. 9. University of Notre Dame Press, 1995) and is reprinted with the permission of the publisher and the editors; Chapter 5 was published in *Revue des Études Augustiniennes* 40 (1994) and is reprinted with the permission of the editors. My thanks are due to all the editors and publishers concerned for permission to reprint these articles here.

The articles have been reprinted virtually as originally

published. I have altered the style of references for the sake of consistency; added translations for Greek and Latin terms in Chapter 3; and a Select Bibliography to Chapter 4. I have not sought to make improvements or to eliminate overlaps, as each chapter was designed to stand by itself, though several deal with problems left on the margins of their predecessors.

Nottingham
November 1995

Chapter One
WORLD AND TEXT IN ANCIENT CHRISTIANITY I: AUGUSTINE

I do not intend in these lectures to do anything so fashionable as to expound whatever semiology or hermeneutics is to be found in the work of early Christian writers. My approach to these things, like theirs, is incorrigibly pre-modern. I shall, however, be touching on matters that fall within the scope of these distinctively modern subjects. For two things, at any rate, are certain: one is that some of the Christian fathers devoted explicit and sophisticated discussion to signs and the way in which they signify. Of these the most notable beyond a doubt is Augustine of Hippo,[1] to whom this first lecture will be devoted, who has even been seen by some modern writers as the father of semiology.[2] The second thing, even less likely

1 For accounts of Augustine's theory of signs, see R. A. Markus, 'Saint Augustine on signs', *Phronesis* 2 (1957) 60–83 (= below, Chapter 3); B. D. Jackson, 'The theory of signs in St Augustine's *De doctrina Christiana*', *REAug* 15 (1969) 9–49 (both reprinted in *Augustine: a collection of critical studies*, ed. R. A. Markus (New York, 1972) 61–91; 92–147); R. A. Markus, 'Signs, Communication and Communities in Augustine's *De doctrina Christiana*', in *De doctrina Christiana: a classic of Western culture*, ed. D. W. H. Arnold and P. Bright (Notre Dame, Indiana, 1995) 97–108 (= below, Chapter 4); T. Todorov, *Théories du symbole* (Paris, 1977) 34–54; most recently, J. M. Rist, *Augustine: Ancient thought baptized* (Cambridge, 1994) 23–40.

2 See, for instance, U. Eco, *Semiotics and the philosophy of language* (London, 1984) 33; R. Simone, 'Sémiologie augustinienne', *Semiotica* 6 (1972) 1–31; T. Todorov, *Théories du symbole* (Paris, 1977) 13; 55–56; 179; S. A. Handelman, *The slayers of Moses: the emergence of Rabbinic interpretation in modern literary theory* (Albany, N.Y., 1982) 107–20; W. Jeanrond, *Theological hermeneutics* (London, 1991) 22. Cf. Averil

to be disputed, is the central place that problems of interpreting the scriptures occupied in their work; almost without exception. Some early Christian writers were very conscious of the theoretical links between these two themes. Again Augustine is our archetypal example of a writer who went to considerable pains to formulate the principles which underlay his exegetical practice; and he did so in terms of a theory of signs. Others were more pragmatic, content to pursue their exegetical practice more unreflectively, leaving the principles in more or less unexplored obscurity. To take just two examples, some two hundred years apart: Jerome and Gregory the Great were very different as exegetes, but neither of them had much interest in exploring or justifying the principles upon which their exegesis proceeded. How they conceived 'meaning' has to be teased out of their texts. How you think of meaning, and how you interpret the meaning of the scriptures: these are the two themes which will lurk behind my lectures. But I want to stress at the outset that they are not what I want to elucidate. Much has been written both on signs and on exegesis, and even though the last word has surely not been said on either, I do not intend to discuss either for their own sake. Rather, I shall be considering how views on the interpretation of the scriptures may have helped to shape views on how to interpret experience more widely. I shall take two examples, some two hundred years apart. In this first lecture I shall consider Augustine of Hippo, writing in the decades around AD 400; and I shall enquire how his views on how the scriptures are to be interpreted determined, or helped to determine, his views of the world around him.

Cameron, *Christianity and rhetoric of empire* (Berkeley, 1991) 227 on Augustine as founder of post-modernism. She refers (n. 4) to A. Kroker [& D. Cook], *The post-modern scene: excremental culture and hyper-aesthetics* (London, 1986) 37, where Augustine is described as the 'Columbus of modern experience'; modern thought is doomed 'to work forever within the Augustinian discourse' (42); modernity begins with Augustine's 'radical reformulation of the philosophy of progress' (57); cf. 59, 61, 72.

God speaks with words and deeds

Put another way, I shall consider the ways in which he read his world in relation to his ways of reading the scriptures. It may seem quaint to speak of 'reading the world'. My warrant for doing so is Augustine's insistence that God speaks not only with words, as do human beings, but also with deeds.[3] There is a problem at the outset: not all that we hear is speech; to understand speech we must be able to distinguish it from the surrounding noise. Augustine, of course, believed that all that is or happens in the world is God's doing; so how did he think we can distinguish the divine speech amid all his deeds, God's *facta*? from everything else that happens? The answer of course is that he thought that there was a particular thread in the history of God's actions: those recorded in the Bible.

Our first approach to this question must be by coming to grips with how Augustine conceived our understanding of God's deeds as recorded in the biblical narratives, for it is in considering how we should go about this that he came to formulate his views about understanding the world around him. That I shall consider when we have examined his views on how God speaks with events contained in the scriptural narratives (see below, pp. 22–31). Though aware of the variety of literary forms in the Bible, Augustine was untroubled by problems about its composite character and its development within a long tradition. The principle he assumed, which in his day would hardly have needed defence, is that the biblical authors are privileged precisely in their narrative function: their selection of the events to be recounted, their way of organising them into a narrative structure, their use of techniques such as cross-reference, repeated patterns and allusion, in short, their 'emplotment', as we might anachronis-

---

3 *Ep.* 102.6.33: *non tantum gesta sed etiam propter aliquam significationem conscripta esse* ... Cf. R. W. Bernard, *In figura: Terminology pertaining to figurative exegesis in the works of Augustine of Hippo* (Dissertation, Princeton, 1984) 186–87 for discussion of this passage.

tically put it. All these 'deeper movements and rhythms' within the text form part of its literal sense.[4]

It may help to illustrate this with an analogy, let us say a narrative of someone going fishing.[5] Such a narrative might include reports of a variety of actions: say, just for the sake of illustration, taking a car out of a garage, putting baskets, sticks, varied strange unknown clutter in the boot, driving a couple of hours, stopping, eating sandwiches, sitting on a river bank holding a stick with a thin string tied to it, sleeping a while and returning to the car and so on. If you are initiated into the angler's intention and the nature of fishing, you will have no difficulty in selecting the individual actions that add up to a narrative of going fishing. You will know how to discern a coherent thread which is only one among a huge range of actions concurrent with those which add up to the 'going fishing', but are not part of it: eating, sleeping, driving, shopping, talking – the multifarious variety of actions that go into daily living, and other projects contemporaneous with the 'going fishing'. If you don't know the unifying intention, you'll be at a loss to construct any narrative; the events which constitute 'going fishing' will be merged and lost among an indefinite multitude of others. Augustine thought of the biblical authors as narrators divinely privileged with an insight which enabled them to discern the thread of what God was *really* up to among all the other things He was busy doing. Their insight enabled them, collectively, to construct a narrative of God's creative and redeeming work. Their text provides us with a 'thick description' of God's work in human history. Augustine assimilated their inspiration to that of the

4 See on this R. D. Williams, 'The literal sense of scripture', *Modern theology* 7 (1991) 121–34.

5 The summary of Augustine's view of the 'inspiration' of the scriptures which follows is based on the fuller account in my *Saeculum: History and society in the theology of Saint Augustine* (Cambridge, 1970; 1989) Appendix A. I speak of biblical narratives here, for the sake of avoiding the complication of non-narrative *genres* in the Bible.

prophets, whose judgements of significance and interpretations of events are made within a divine perspective and carry, for the peoples of the Book, a warrant of divine authority. It is by virtue of their inclusion within the biblical narratives that we both know that the constituent events of the narrative have a meaning, and that we can get to know what that meaning is, by attending to the clues furnished within the biblical narrative taken as a whole.

What it is critically important to note is that Augustine is insisting that not only does the biblical author's text have a meaning, but that what that text refers to, the things or events it tells of, can also have their meaning. Thus of a verse of Genesis he says: 'this was done for the sake of signifying something; but done it was, just as things said for the sake of signifying something are said'. He continues, apologising for being tiresomely insistent: 'as I have often said, and as I never tire of saying, what we expect of a narrator of historical events is that he should narrate what has been done as facts, and what has been said as sayings. Just as concerning deeds we can ask [two different questions]: what was done, and what does it signify?, so also concerning words: what was said, and what does it mean? Whether that which is recorded to have been said was said figuratively or literally, the statement recording its saying is not to be taken figuratively.'[6] Augustine is insisting here on the literal meaning of the biblical narrator's

---

6 *De Gen. ad litt.* XI.39.52: *Et hoc significationis gratia factum est, sed tamen factum; sicut illa quae significationis gratia dicta sunt, sed tamen dicta sunt. Hoc enim, quod saepe dixi nec me saepius piget dicere, a narratore rerum proprie gestarum exigendum est, ut ea narret facta esse quae facta sunt, et dicta esse quae dicta sunt. Sicut autem in factis quaeritur quid factum sit, et quid significet; ita in verbis et quid dictum sit, et quid significet. Sive enim figurate sive proprie dictum sit, quod dictum esse narratur, dictum tamen esse non debet putari figuratum.* Cf. among others: *De doctr. Christ.* I.2.2; II.10.15; *Enarr. in Ps.* 113.i.1; *C. Faust.* XII.40; *De ciu. Dei* XV.27. For the care Augustine takes to distinguish this kind of figurative text from allegory, see the text referred to in the next note.

report, whether it reports words or deeds; and he draws our attention to the principle he often states, that the scriptural author is telling of God's mighty – and meaningful – deeds, and that what he reports is to be taken literally. We may take as illustrative his remarks on the exposition of Genesis 2:9, 'the tree of life also in the midst of the garden, and the tree of the knowledge of good and evil':

> It is to be carefully considered, lest we be driven into allegory, that these were not in fact trees, but that something else is signified by the word 'tree'. For it is said of Wisdom, 'She is a tree of life to those who lay hold of her' (Prov. 3:18). Indeed, although the eternal Jerusalem is in heaven, the city whereby it is signified is one built on earth; and similarly Sarah and Hagar, although they signify the two Covenants, were also two women; and as Christ waters us by the spiritual spring of his suffering on the cross, He was also the rock which gave water to the thirsting people when struck by a rod; hence it could be said 'and the Rock was Christ' (1 Cor. 10:4). All these signified something other than themselves, yet they were themselves what they were. And when they are spoken of by the narrator, that is not figurative expression, but literal mention of things which prefigure . . . The story itself is about [things which are] figures; it is not a figurative expression about things [i.e. parables and other metaphorical speech].[7]

It is the Lord of history who so disposes events that they 'signify' – or, as I shall sometimes say, in line with Augustine's

---

7 *De Gen. ad litt.* VIII.4.8: *diligentius considerandum est, ne cogat in allegoriam, ut non ista ligna fuerint, sed aliud aliquid nomine ligni significent. Dictum est enim de sapientia, Lignum vitae est omnibus amplectentibus eam. Verumtamen cum sit Jerusalem aeterna in caelis, etiam in terra civitas qua illa significaretur condita est; et Sara et Agar quamvis duo testamenta significarent, erant tamen quaedam etiam mulieres duae; et cum Christus per ligni passionem fluento spirituali nos irriget, erat tamen et petra,*

usage, 'prefigure' – other events. That significance is revealed to us, or at least we are given clues to it, in the biblical narrative taken as a whole. The clue may be distant; it may not be within the text before us, or even within its immediate context. We may have to search in St Paul as to what was prefigured by a commandment first given – and to be taken literally! – by Moses; and, to take a central example, the great events of the Exodus find their meaning disclosed in the redemption wrought by Christ.[8] These things or events derive their significance 'not from the facts themselves, but from God's almighty wisdom';[9] such things were done *propter aliquam significationem.*[10] So Adam, or the Suffering Servant, figuratively signify Christ, and Elijah John the Baptist, because the New Testament presents Christ or John the Baptist in such guise. As the late Austin Farrer remarked, 'It was possible for Christ and the Apostles to use the images [he is referring to the "great images", the figure of the Son of Man, the ceremony of the sacramental body, the bloody sacrifice of the Lamb, the enthronement of the Anointed] meaningfully, because the old archetypes were there to hand . . . Christ clothed himself in

---

quae aquam sitienti populo ligno percussa manavit, de qua diceretur, Petra autem erat Christus. Aliud quam erant illa omnia significaverunt, sed tamen etiam ipsa corporaliter fuerunt. Et quando a narrante commemorata sunt, non erat illa figurata locutio, sed earum rerum expressa narratio, quarum erat figurata praecessio . . . ipsa narratio figurarum est, non rerum figurata significatio gestarum.

8 The example of Deut. 25:4 and I Cor. 9:9; I Tim. 5:18 ('Thou shalt not muzzle the ox that treadeth out the corn') is used by Augustine in *De doctr. Christ.* II.10.15; *Enarr. in Ps.* 65.20; 102.12; 103.iii.9; 126.11; 145.13; *De op. mon.* 7.8; *C. Faust.* VI.9 etc. On Exodus, a particularly instructive passage: *Enarr. in Ps.* 113.i.1.

9 *De Gen. ad litt.* XI.34.45: *haec mysticis significationibus plena sunt non id agentibus in quibus facta sunt, sed de his agente potentissima sapientia Dei;* cf. the parallel passages cited by Solignac, *Oeuvres de Saint Augustin: La Genèse au sens litéral,* ed. P. Agaësse & A. Solignac (*BA* 48, 49, Paris, 1972) 1.37 n. 70.

10 *De Gen. ad litt.,* IX.12.20.

the archetypal images, and then began to do and to suffer.'[11] The prefigured becomes part of the sense – let us, in line with modern usage, call it 'typological' – of the prefiguring. To unravel this meaning the interpreter needs, of course, to possess a general knowledge of the sacred history, that is to say of the particular passage in the context of the whole Bible.[12] In principle, at any rate, the clue to figurative meaning must lie in the biblical narrative, no less than do the clues to literal meaning. This must be so because it is the facts which are God's speech that are given their meaning by divine semantic intention, mediated by the (prophetically inspired) biblical author and disclosed in the biblical discourse: 'One and the same Spirit is at work in the things done and the things said'.[13]

The retreat from allegory

It is important not to mistake what Augustine is asserting in this theory of divine communication, for it distinguishes his account of it from a well-established tradition of allegorical interpretation from Clement of Alexandria to Ambrose. And it is all the more important to appreciate the gulf that separates Augustine from that tradition because he is not at all clear or consistent in the way he uses the terms 'figure' and 'allegory'

11 A. Farrer, *The Glass of Vision* (London, 1948) 109; 146. Cf. G. W. H. Lampe, 'The reasonableness of Typology', in G. W. H. Lampe & K. J. Woolcombe, *Essays on Typology* (Studies in Biblical Theology, 22. London, 1957) 29.

12 As M. Irvine, *The making of textual culture* (Cambridge, 1994) remarks, of Origen's typological sense: '[it] involves not merely an additional meaning [as does the allegorical sense] but the constitution of a new sign from the referent in the narrative of sacred history' (254). This corresponds to Augustine's exactly: cf. *ibid.*, 262, referred to below, n. 20. See also Bernard, *In figura*, 174, 192.

13 *Enarr. in Ps.* 113.i.1: *Uno eodemque Spiritu operante et illa facta et haec dicta . . .*

and their cognates;[14] nor is he by any means consistently faithful to his own theory in his exegetical practice, but in fact shows himself capable of quite as baroque extravagance in some of his comments as any that might be found in Clement or Ambrose.

Our age is temperamentally predisposed to deny the possibility of any authoritative reading of texts. The same was also true of Augustine's; but in a very different way. Our predicament springs from a belief in the autonomy of the reader, the question mark that it places over the authority of the text. In Late Antiquity the problem was the opposite. Readers saw themselves as wholly subject to the texts they took as authoritative; and texts were seen as authoritative in only too many ways: as sources of doctrine, as models of style, as sanctioning cult, as the fountainheads of living traditions. Whether the text was that of Homer, of Virgil or the Bible, sanction for belief and practice was sought in the canonised text. But this had important consequences for the way these texts were understood. If their authority was to remain unassailable, great latitude had to be preserved for scope in interpreting what they said. If a late Roman man of letters wanted to find the source of his devotion in Virgil, he would need to allow himself the degree of freedom in interpreting the *Aeneid* that was countenanced by, for example, Macrobius. Allegorical reading was the accepted means whereby a text could be given a meaning other than its 'literal' meaning, thereby securing the necessary freedom in interpreting the text.[15] No very clear distinction was generally made between an allegorical text and allegorical interpretation. Allegorising

14 I give only a few, especially significant, examples. The fullest exposition of all this now is Bernard, *In figura*.

15 See, J. Pépin, *Mythe et allégorie* (Paris, 1958), and, most recently, the widely ranging discussion by R. Lamberton, *Homer the theologian: Neoplatonist allegorical reading and the growth of the tradition* (Berkeley, California, 1986).

was a means of making a text say something other than what it was obviously saying.

Like any trained grammarian, Augustine knew the ancient usage according to which allegory was an extended metaphor.[16] But he felt ill at ease with the received usage; he was 'dependent upon an inherited tradition that he [found] not to be entirely satisfactory'.[17] He wanted to define a figurative sense which was not allegorical, and he laid the theoretical foundations for doing so in his work, the *De doctrina Christiana*. What he discovered and elaborated in the account of signs which he gave in this work is that a text can be taken in its strictest literal meaning and may nevertheless have, indirectly, a further reference. It is the events narrated by it that may themselves have a meaning, that is to say, they constitute, as he said, a divine discourse.[18] It is not the biblical text that means something other than what it appears on the face of it to be saying. It is what the text is literally referring to that itself has a further meaning. Augustine calls the signs used by the biblical writers in recording such discourse *signa translata*, and he defines them as signs which occur when 'the things signified by their proper literal names are in their turn used to signify something else'.[19] 'Figurative signs', as I shall call *signa translata*, seem therefore to be ordinary names or expressions whose literal meaning is, so to speak, short-circuited in this

16 *De Trin.* XV.9.15: *tropus ubi ex alio aliud intelligitur.*

17 Bernard, *In figura*, 108, to whose magisterial discussion of this subject (105–56) I owe much.

18 See above, n. 3. Augustine often emphasises that it is the facts that have meaning: e.g. *De Trin.* XV.9.15: when St Paul (Gal. 4:24) says of Abraham's two sons 'now this is an allegory', *ubi allegoriam nominavit apostolus, non in verbis eam reperit sed in facto . . .*

19 *De doctr. Christ.* II.10.15: *translata sunt [signa] cum et ipsae res quas propriis verbis significamus, ad aliud aliquid significandum usurpantur . . .* Cf. the distinction in I.2.2 between *res* which *non ad significandum aliud adhibentur . . .* and *res* which *ita res sunt ut aliarum etiam signa sunt rerum . . .*

kind of discourse, and whose final referents are the more remote events or objects signified by the (by-passed) immediate referents.[20] This can be schematically represented thus:

A: Sign (word) → Signified (thing, event)

B: Sign (word) → Signified$_1$ (thing, event)$_1$→ Signified$_2$

[Transferred sign = Sign + signified$_1$]   → Signified$_2$

where A represents the normal relationships of signification

and B represents the relationships in the case of 'transferred' signs

Augustine gives the example of the word 'ox'. Used literally the word signifies the beast. It is the beast referred to by the word in its literal sense which, in its turn, refers, as a sign, to 'something else', in this case the evangelist. It is this double relationship of signification that is condensed in the 'transferred' or 'figurative' sense which accrues to the word when used in the appropriate scriptural context.

This was the foundation of a clear distinction between 'typological' and other kinds of 'figurative' or allegorical senses. Like many modern scholars, I shall credit Augustine with having made this distinction, even though in his practice it is often blurred. Types, on this usage, will be events, persons or episodes in the sacred history which point to a future 'antitype'; allegories, or other figures, lack such a historical foundation in facts; they are based only on words. Typological interpretation always presupposes a literal sense; allegory can by-pass it.[21]

20 Bernard, *In figura*, 54–55 uses the schema, derived from Augustine, of *signum, res significans, res significata (aliud aliquid)*. In 'figurative' discourse the middle term is passed over, the *signum translatum* being used to signify the *aliud aliquid*. See also Irvine, *Making of textual culture*, 262–63.

21 See for instance Bernard, *In figura*, 158–64; Irvine, *The making* (257–62) is less aware of development in Augustine's views, but provides a clear account of the distinction between typological and allegorical signification: 'Augustine . . . [distinguishes] between allegory [*De Trin.* XV.9.15; cf. *De doctr. Christ.* III.29.40–41] and typology, that is, figurative expressions

Textual constraint and exegetical freedom

Like many Christian writers before him, and many more later, Augustine knew very well – as did Jerome – the difference between strict textual restraint and the freedom of allegorical interpretation.[22] If God speaks to men, it is rather important to listen to Him and not to put words in His mouth; so unrestrained allegorising must be ruled out. This is exactly what Augustine's distinction between typological and allegorical senses of a passage was designed to do, and this is his overriding purpose, even when he appears to be in breach of his own principles.

Augustine's exegetical practice, however, is much less clear than his view on how God speaks. His uncertain terminology and his erratic, often lyrical, playful or extravagant exegeses[23] blur the theoretical distinction he made so clearly. The old, discarded practice, and the theoretical uncertainty underlying it, continued to colour Augustine's later practice, even though beyond any doubt he felt increasingly uneasy about allegory.[24] He wanted some means of reconciling the possibility of texts bearing more than their single, literal meaning with the interpreter's strict subjection to the authority of the text; but

---

(simple tropes) and statements which refer to people or events in sacred history which in turn are signs of other things in subsequent history' (259).

22 Jerome, *Comm. in proph. min., In Abac.* I.1.6.11: *historia stricta est, et evagandi non habet facultatem; tropologia libera, et his tantum legibus circumscripta, ut pietatem servatur intellegentiae* . . . referred to by H. de Lubac, *Exégèse médiévale* 1 (Paris, 1959) 43–44, who gives a brief survey of the Patristic evidence. For a modern discussion of this theme, see the essays in *Textual determinacy* Part I, ed. R. C. Culley & R. B. Robinson, *Semeia* 62 (1993).

23 Of which H.-I. Marrou has given a handsome defence in the *Retractatio* (1949) to his *St Augustin et la fin de la culture antique* (1938) 646–51; repeating, however, that he discusses the matter not 'en elle-même, mais seulement pour ses implications culturelles' (647); cf. 492. This is not the place to consider examples of Augustine's exegesis; see M. Pontet, *L'exégèse de Saint Augustin prédicateur* (Paris, 1946).

24 See Bernard, *In figura*, 105–56.

he continued to take liberties with the text unsupported by his own principles.

This exegetical freedom is hardly surprising. Augustine had availed himself of it generously in the years just preceding the writing of the *De doctrina Christiana*. The Manichees rejected anything but rigidly literal exposition of the scriptures. It was Ambrose's 'spiritual' exposition[25] that liberated Augustine from the Manichees' literalism, and with it, from their rejection of the absurdities, as they saw them, of the Old Testament.[26] In his polemical works directed against his former fellow-Manichees, as, for instance, in his *De Genesi contra Manichaeos*, Augustine had made liberal use of the exegetical procedures he had learned from Ambrose. He had tried to take the text (especially of Genesis 2–3) literally but found himself unable to make sense of it, so (as he recalled later) he turned to the 'allegorical mode of expression'.[27] He gladly invoked the authority of the Pauline verse 'The letter killeth, but the Spirit giveth life' (2 Cor. 3:6) to allow himself the utmost freedom in expounding the scriptures.[28]

But Augustine changed his mind on this, as on so many things. The verse, he wrote later, should not be understood to mean that something that looks absurd should be 'taken in a sense other than its literal meaning, taking it to mean something else'. Rather, he now thought, it should be understood to say that 'the letter of the Law which teaches that we should not sin, kills when the life-giving Spirit is lacking'.[29] Step by

25 On Ambrose, see H. Savon, 'Maniérisme et allégorie dans l'oeuvre d'Ambroise de Milan', *REL* 55 (1977) 203–21.

26 His own account is given in *Conf.* VI (see especially 4.6). On it see the comment by J. J. O'Donnell, *Augustine: Confessions* (Oxford, 1992) 2, 350f. For the *Confessions* I have used O'Donnell's text (vol. 1). See also *De util. cred.* 8.20.

27 *De Gen. ad litt.* VIII.2.5: *non secundum allegoricam locutionem* . . .

28 *Conf.* VI.4.6; *De doctr. Christ.* III.5.9 etc.

29 On Augustine's second thoughts on this verse, originally used to justify allegorical exegesis (in his early work): *Retract.* I.14.1 with *De util. cred.* 3.9 and *De spir. et litt.* 4.6–5.8, from which the quotations in the text

step, in the mid- and late 390s, Augustine moved away from his previous position. From the start of his ecclesiastical career, Augustine had been serious about understanding the text of the scriptures, rather than using it. When he asked his bishop for time off to allow him to equip himself better for his ministry, at the time of his ordination to the priesthood, Augustine was no novice, either to the Bible, or to the techniques of expounding texts. He was well aware that the training of a late Roman rhetor had not equipped him for the work of a Christian pastor: 'in truth, I did not yet know what I was lacking for such a task [the ministry of the sacraments and the word of God] . . .'[30] We should notice, however, what is often overlooked: that even in his letter of application for study-leave, he was not asking simply for time to study the scriptures. He knew enough for his own salvation, he dared to affirm; what he needed to acquire was 'what I lack in order to minister to the salvation of others; "not seeking my own profit, but the profit of many, that they may be saved" (1 Cor. 10:33)'.[31] From the very start of his clerical career, what exercised Augustine's mind was not so much the question how the biblical text was to be understood, but how it was to be expounded in the believing community.

Not long after entering on his ministry, he began a protracted, and notorious, correspondence with Jerome.[32]

---

are taken. It was of course the Pelagian controversy that gave this interpretation its force: see e.g. *Sermo* 251.6; *De gratia et de pecc. orig.* I.8.9. For contrast with Gregory's usage, see Chapter 2, n. 43.

30 *Ep.* 21.3: *quod verum est, nondum sciebam, quid mihi deesset ad tale opus . . . quid sit homini necessarium qui populo ministrat sacramentum et verbum dei . . .*

31 *Ep.* 21.4: *Auderem enim dicere scire me et plena fide retinere quid pertineat ad salutem nostram. Sed hoc ipsum quomodo ministrem ad salutem aliorum: non quaerens quod mihi utile est, sed quod multis, ut salvi fiant.*

32 Among other accounts, see G. Strauss, *Schriftgebrauch, Schriftauslegung und Schriftbeweis bei Augustin* (Beitr. z. Gesch. d. biblischen Hermeneutik 1. Tübingen, 1959) 45–46; and J. N. D. Kelly, *Jerome: his life, writings, and controversies* (London, 1975) 217–18; 263–72. Most recently,

Several issues were at stake: Jerome's use of the Hebrew text of the Old Testament rather than the LXX and the current Latin versions; and, especially, interpreting the scriptures (Gal. 2.11–21) in a manner that might imply an apostle not speaking the truth.[33] Behind this ostensible point of contention, however, Augustine saw a further, and more fundamental issue: once the possibility of apostolic dissimulation is admitted, 'the authority of the divine scriptures is so undermined that anyone can find there what he wants to believe and to reject what he does not want to believe . . .'[34] Lies are to be feared as 'the worm of doubt which gnaws away at the literal meaning of all the scripture . . .'[35] What concerned Augustine was, above all, the authority of the text.

This concern also underlies a great part of the discussion in a work that Augustine began very soon after embarking on his correspondence with Jerome, the *De doctrina Christiana*. To make explicit the rules which should govern the exposition of the scriptures appears, in fact, to be one of his primary aims: 'There are certain precepts for treating the scriptures . . .', as the much-debated Prologue to the work begins;[36] and rules

---

F. Dolbeau, 'Sermons inédits de Saint Augustin prêchés en 397 (2ème série)', *RBen* 102 (1991) 44–74, at 47–48, where full references are given.

33 *Ep.* 28.3.

34 *Ibid.*, 3.5: . . . *cognoscis fluctuare auctoritatem divinarum scripturarum ut in eis, quod vult quisque credat, quod non vult non credat, si semel fuerit persuasum aliqua illos viros per quos nobis ministrata sunt in scripturis suis officiosis potuisse mentiri . . .*; cf. *De doctr. Christ.* III.27.38; *C. Faust.* XI.2; XXXII.19; *Ep.* 147.40.

35 *Sermo Dolbeau* 10.13: *tamquam vermiculus malignus ad omnem scripturae rodendum litteram metuendus . . .* Dolbeau, 'Sermons inédits' (as in n. 32, above) 61.

36 *De doctr. Christ.*, Prol.: *Sunt praecepta quaedam tractandarum scripturarum . . .* (*CC* 32, 1, l.1). Of the large literature on the Prologue and the purpose of the work, see: P. Brunner, 'Charismatische und methodische Schriftauslegung nach Augustins Prolog zu «De doctrina Christiana»', *Kerygma und Dogma* 1 (1955) 59–69, 85–103; J. Martin, 'Abfassung, Veröffentlichung und Überlieferung von Augustins Schrift «De doctrina Christiana»', *Traditio* 18 (1962) 69–87; U. Duchrow, 'Zum Prolog von

still preoccupied Augustine when he came to complete the
interrupted work thirty years later, and included in his treatise
the Rules for interpreting the scriptures listed by Tyconius.
The exegete's freedom – whatever may be its limits – must not
be arbitrary, but subject to rules. This concern for rules
springs from Augustine's consciousness of a tension between
the absolute authority of what the text says, and the freedom
he had discovered in the work of the exegete. He found
himself wanting to take the literal sense of the text he was
expounding as seriously as the 'spiritual'; and, eventually, to
give the literal absolute precedence.[37] Whatever else the *De
doctrina Christiana* was designed to clear up, Augustine must
certainly have expected to clear up in it the hermeneutic
principles implicit in his, and others', exegetical practice.

Authorial intention

Augustine began the *De doctrina Christiana* with a distinction
between two things involved in 'all treatment of the scriptures:
the way of discovery of what is to be understood, and the way
of expressing what has been understood',[38] that is to say with
seeking to understand, and with communicating that which
had been understood, in both cases, clearly, the scriptures.

Augustins *De doctrina christiana*', *VigChr* 17 (1963) 165–72; E. Kevane,
'Paideia and anti-paideia: the Proemium of St Augustine's «De doctrina
christiana»', *AugSt* 1 (1970) 153–80; *id.*, 'Augustine's «De doctrina christiana»: a treatise on Christian education', *RechAug* 4 (1966) 97–133; L. M. J.
Verheijen, 'Le *De doctrina Christiana* de saint Augustin. Un manuel
d'herméneutique et d'expression chrétienne avec, en II.19.29–42.63, une
«charte fondamentale pour une culture chrétienne»', *Augustiniana* 24 (1974)
10–20; C. P. Mayer, '«Res per signa»: Der Grundgedanke des Prologs in
Augustins Schrift *De doctrina Christiana* und das Problem seiner Datierung', *REAug* 20 (1974) 100–12.

37 On this development, see Bernard, *In figura*, 105–56.

38 *De doctr. Christ.* I.1.1: *Duae sunt res quibus nititur omnis tractatio
scripturarum: modus inveniendi quae intellegenda sunt, et modus proferendi
quae intellecta sunt.* Cf. IV.1.1.

This signposts the contents of Books II–III and of Book IV respectively. But what about Book I? Augustine's answer to the question is that it is concerned with *doctrina* about *things* (*res*), whereas the rest deals with *signs*: the two classes of objects that *doctrina* can be about.[39] This raises more questions than it answers, but this is not the place to discuss, yet again, the vexed question of what precisely the extended and important discussion of the structuring of human love (in terms of the conceptual pair of *uti* and *frui*) which constitutes the substance of Book I has to do with the rest of the work, concerned with exactly what Augustine says at the outset, the understanding and the communication of the meaning of the scriptures.[40] For our purpose, however, the transitional chapters which serve as a bridge between Book I and the sequel are crucially important.

Augustine has completed his discussion of the theme of Book I: what is to be loved and how human love is to be structured in terms of the double command of charity; for this is the whole aim and substance of the scriptures.[41] Now, before he sets out on the next stage of his enquiry: how is the meaning of scripture to be ascertained?, he deals with the preliminary questions: what are the limits within which we may look for an answer? and what can be ruled out in advance? And to these questions he is now in a position to give a clear answer: any interpretation that breaches the command of charity cannot be a correct understanding. This may look like

39 *De doctr. Christ.* I.2.2.

40 See the text referred to in n. 38.

41 *De doctr. Christ.* I.35.39; cf. II.7.10. I do not discuss here the final paragraphs of Book I, 38.42–40.44. They concern either those who already are firm in faith, hope and charity, and do not need to expound the scriptures to others (are these the charismatic interpreters who had no use for disciplined exegesis hinted at in the Prologue – as argued e.g. by Duchrow, 'Zum Prolog' and Kevane, 'Paideia and anti-paideia', above, n. 36 – or those who enjoy the heavenly vision? Neither category is in need of the painstaking discipline of studying the rules of correct exegesis.)

no more than a negative criterion, ruling out any exegesis which fails to meet it. But the charity Augustine has in mind is a love formed by faith. He is insisting that interpreting any individual text presupposes some kind of grasp of the overall meaning of the biblical revelation.[42] Charity – our love of God and neighbour – is what it is, in the end, all about: the meaning of any part cannot contradict the meaning of the whole. The criterion of charity is therefore crucially important, even if it does not actually help the exegete in his immediate task of elucidating a particular text. Augustine is careful to acknowledge this when he goes on to say that a particular exegesis may serve the law of charity, but it may nevertheless be mistaken; not culpably, but all the same, arriving at the right destination by a wrong route. And habitual taking of the wrong route, he says, can be dangerous.[43] To understand the text, he insists, is to read it in accordance with its author's intention. The scriptures were spread throughout the world in the various languages of their translators 'so that they might profitably become known to all the peoples for their salvation, who, reading them, wished to discover nothing other than the thoughts and intentions of those who wrote them, and through them, the will of God, according to which we believe their authors to have spoken'.[44]

But it is the nature of authors to be elusive, and of the scriptural authors above all. 'Moses wrote this; he wrote and went his way . . .':[45] the author has gone, the text alone remains. Augustine's insistence on the primacy of authorial intention has been obscured by the fact that he frequently

---

42 See above, n. 12.

43 *De doctr. Christ.* I.36.40–41.

44 *De doctr. Christ.* I.5.6: *per varias interpretum linguas longe lateque diffusa innotesceret gentibus ad salutem, quam legentes nihil aliud appetunt quam cogitationes voluntatemque illorum a quibus conscripta est, invenire et per illas voluntatem Dei, secundum quam tales homines locutos esse credimus*; cf. I.37.41.

45 *Conf.* XI.3.5: *Scripsit hoc Moyses, scripsit et abiit . . .*

defends the 'polysemy of scripture and licit plurality of interpretation'.[46] In the *Confessions*, in the course of what is his most extensive discussion (XII.14.17–26.36) of the subject, Augustine seems, in fact, to be facing in two different directions. He has been meditating on the opening verses of Genesis (to XII.15.22); he has found Genesis to be subject to a wide variety of interpretations, even among just those who accept it as supremely authoritative.[47] So he must now launch into a discussion as to how to discriminate between alternative interpretations of a text accepted as authoritative. He concludes:

> As long as each interpreter is endeavouring to find in the holy scriptures the meaning of the author who wrote it, what evil is it if an exegesis he gives is one shown to be true by You [God], light of all sincere souls, even if the author whom he is reading did not have that idea and, though he had grasped a truth, had not discerned that seen by the interpreter?[48]

This is in line with the view put forward in the *De doctrina Christiana*: we must seek the meaning intended by the author

46 I take the phrase from O'Donnell, 3.316. See pp. 317, 326–27, 341 for his discussion of this question. B. De Margerie, *Introduction to the history of exegesis. III: St Augustine* (E. trans. Petersham, Mass., 1993) 47–88 as far as I can understand it, seems to arrive at a conclusion similar to mine. His meaning is not always beyond doubt; he speaks of 'orderly polysemy' (55), 'unified polysemy' (77), 'transcendent verbal occasionalism' and 'uniplural-ism' (60).

47 *Conf.* XII.16.23. On *culmen auctoritatis* see O'Donnell, 2.353–54. The older analysis by A. Solignac in *Oeuvres de Saint Augustin. Les Confessions* (*BA* 14. Paris, 1962) 609–12 follows similar lines.

48 *Conf.* XII.18.27: *id sentire in scripturis sanctis quod in eis sensit ille qui scripsit, quid mali est hoc sentiat quod tu, lux omnium veridicarum mentium, ostendis verum esse, etiamsi non hoc sensit ille quem legit, cum et ille verum nec tamen hoc senserit?* (trans. Chadwick, 259–60. The translations of all quotations from the *Confessions* in the text are from that of H. Chadwick (Oxford, 1991); page references are given to this.)

but we shall not offend the law of charity if we fail in that quest; we will have arrived at the right destination by the wrong route. As Augustine's most faithful and most meticulous commentator remarks: 'Seeking the author's intention is legitimate [for "legitimate" I would say, with Augustine, "desirable", or even, "obligatory"], but missing it is legitimate as well. This does not detach the text from the author's intention . . .'[49] Augustine knew very well how fragile and unreliable was the link between reader and author: only God's illuminative presence in our minds can resolve the ambiguities and the uncertainties inherent in our present condition.[50] Aware of the polysemy of signs, he distinguishes two kinds of question that a text may raise:

> The first concerns the truth of the matter in question. The second concerns the intention of the writer. It is one thing to enquire into the truth about the origin of the creation. It is another to ask what understanding of the words on the part of a reader and hearer was intended by Moses . . .[51]

Nothing could be clearer than this emphatic discrimination between two different enterprises, which we might, for convenience, call the exegetical in a strict sense, and the interpretative, that is to say exposition of a truth related in some other way to the text in question. For the present, I shall

49 O'Donnell, 3.326. The rest of the comment (326–27) on the passage forms the subject of my discusssion in the sequel.

50 *Conf.* XIII.14.15 (O'Donnell, 189): *inter quos et nos in isto adhuc incerto humanae notitiae tu solus dividis, qui probas corda nostra et vocas lucem diem et tenebras noctem* . . . See O'Donnell, 3.327, who refers in this connection to *Conf.* X.3.3.

51 *Conf.* XII.23.32: *duo video dissensionum genera oboriri posse cum aliquid a nuntiis veracibus per signa enuntiatur: unum, si de veritate rerum, alterum, si de ipsius qui enuntiat voluntate dissensio est. aliter enim quaerimus de creaturae conditione quid verum sit, aliter autem quid in his verbis Moyses . . . intellegere lectorem auditoremque voluerit.*

keep to the kind of activity I have labelled 'exegetical'; I shall
consider the activity distinguished from it by Augustine,
which I have labelled 'interpretative', later (below, p. 35).

The ensuing discussion, however, confuses the issue and
raises a doubt as to Augustine's commitment to the text and its
author's intention as the criterion for assessing an interpretation. In XII.25.35–26.36 he appears to be saying that he
would like to think that Moses had been inspired to allow, in a
concise expression, for all the variety of interpretations
offered by exegetes with true opinions (on related questions,
such as the theology of creation).[52] A little later he is driven to
confess that faced with this 'diversity of true statements'
concerning the creation, if asked which was the view of Moses
himself, he would have to reply: 'I don't know'.[53] Note that
neither here, nor anywhere else, does Augustine assert that all
the true interpretations advanced were intended by the author
and are part of the meaning of the text, though he comes
sufficiently close to doing so to have misled some of his
commentators. In the following paragraph he asks (a rare lapse
into optimism!) for mutual tolerance among rival exegetes; it
is, however, a tolerance based on compromising textual
constraint on the interpreter: 'why not believe that Moses
discerned all these things [the endless variety of different
views]?' – maybe God did inspire him to write a text which
could embrace them all. Augustine endorses exegetical free-
wheeling among multiple meanings only when the author's
intended meaning cannot be discovered: then we can resort to
giving 'a plurality of meanings to a single obscure expression
in a text we have read'.[54]

Like Origen, Augustine was bewildered by the apparent
ease with which interpretations could proliferate. He was

52 Augustine restates this view in XII.31.42.
53 *Conf.* XII.30.41.
54 *Conf.* XII.24.37: . . . *multis modis intellegere quod obscure uno modo
enuntiatum legerimus* (trans. Chadwick, 296). Cf. *De doctr. Christ.*
III.27.38.

tempted to justify such unlimited semiosis on the grounds that
human speech and understanding are too weak to exhaust the
meaning of the scriptural text.[55] Words fail against the greater
silences; the mystery abides. 'The clearer this appears to me',
Augustine said of a psalm he was expounding, 'the more
profound it tends to seem, to the extent that I cannot even show
how profound it is.'[56] But, again like Origen, Augustine saw
the necessity for restricting the multiplicity of interpretations.
The text may have depths that human discourse cannot plumb;
it may be that several alternative readings break its richness into
manageable fragments; but in the end, this 'semiotic anxiety' is
allayed by the assurance that the text does have a definite, if
unattainable, meaning, which will be manifested to him who
knocks.[57] And this remains the burden of the prayer with
which Augustine closes Book XII, and, indeed, of his subsequent statements on this subject.[58] They all amount to the
assertion that the text has *a* meaning (with sometimes a further
one built upon this, as we have seen) which the exegete should
seek, and many meanings which others – Augustine is usually
thinking of true believers – may find.

Subjection to signs

To summarise this first point in my argument: according to
Augustine's account, God can speak with things by disposing
them in appropriate ways, and inspiring His privileged nar-

55 Irvine, *The making*, 265–71: 'the biblical text is a vast field of signs so
constituted by its rhetoric to be forever indicating its own insufficiency as
the univocal statement of the Logos' (265).

56 *Enarr. in Ps.* 118, prooem., referred to by O'Donnell, *Augustine's
Confessions*, 3.316 as a parallel to *Conf.* XII.14.17.

57 *Conf.* XIII.28.53; on 'semiotic anxiety' see Irvine, *The making*,
265–71.

58 E.g. *De Gen. ad litt.* I.21.41: *aliud est enim quid potissimum scriptor
senserit non dinoscere, aliud autem a regula pietatis errare . . . De doctr.
Christ.* III.27.38 (of 426). Echoes in many other passages, e.g. *De ciu. Dei*
XX.1.1: the scripture is to be understood as meant.

rators to construct their narrative in such a way as to make His meaning clear, or at least to give sufficient hints to provide gainful employment to an army of biblical scholars. But, to come to the next stage in my argument, Augustine was clear that God's speech might fail to communicate; or, in Ricoeurian terms, they can fail to become realised as discourse.[59] To understand the biblical narrative you must know its language; to understand it as revealing divine communication through deeds also requires the right sort of reader: one who will be prepared to discern through the *eloquentia* of the biblical author the *divina eloquentia*.[60] Readers who refuse to see the linguistic function of these things or events, Augustine identifies as 'captive' to the letter, or to 'carnal understanding'. Such a reader, he says 'follows the letter, taking figurative words as literal, refusing to allow a further reference to something else in that which is literally signified by a word: as, for example, hearing the word "sabbath", he understands it to mean only one of the seven days of the week that come round in regular sequence; . . . it is a miserable servitude of the mind to take signs for things . . .'[61] Augustine insists that not knowing the meaning of a sign is not of itself servitude: what is servitude is to enclose oneself in a restricted discourse, refusing to entertain the possibility of piercing the opacity of a sign, and to cut

59 Especially: P. Ricoeur, 'The hermeneutical function of distanciation', 'What is a text? Explanation and understanding', and 'The model of the text. Meaningful action considered as text', in *From text to action* (Evanston, Ill., 1991) 75–88, 105–43 and 144–67. Augustine saw the Bible as the place where God 'converses' with men: *ibi [in firmamento scripturae tuae] enim nobiscum disputas Conf.* XIII.18.22.

60 *divina eloquentia: Ep.* 102.6.33; *C. Faust.* XXI.10.

61 *De doctr. Christ.* III.5.9: *qui enim sequitur litteram, translata verba sicut propria tenet, neque illud quod proprio verbo significatur, refert ad alium significationem: sed si sabbatum audierit, verbi gratia, non intelligit nisi unum diem de septem, qui continuo volumine repetuntur . . . Ea demum est miserabilis animae servitus, signa pro rebus accipere.* The discussion, with particular attention given to distinguishing Jewish from pagan 'captivity to the sign', extends to 9.13.

off the range of potential further meaning it can have in a larger discourse.[62] It is this opening into a new realm of meaning that Augustine has in mind when he says that 'Christian freedom has liberated those it found in subjection to (useful) signs . . . by raising them, through interpreting the signs to which they were subject, to the things of which those signs were the signs'.[63]

We shall have to explore further the important questions raised by Augustine's insistence that understanding a text requires the right sort of reader. But let us pause for a moment at this point, to recall that Augustine had devised this elaborate account of signs and meaning contained in his *De doctrina Christiana* for the purpose of explaining the meaning of biblical signs. In all this Augustine has in mind God's *facta* recorded in the Old Testament. It was from this beginning that his concern with signs grew into something of far wider application – first, under the immediate pressures of controversy, into helping him formulate his theology of the sacraments,[64] and, gradually, into wider areas yet.[65] Naturally, therefore, when Augustine was busy exploring the principles of interpreting signs, the world of biblical signs had the central place in his thinking; and especially those which had the most interesting and richest range of possible meanings, the signs of the Old Testament. Hence also the prominence he gave to the Jews here, the people who were blind to the truth when shown it. They are Augustine's hermeneutical

62 *De doctr. Christ.* III.9.13: *qui autem non intelligit quid significet signum, et tamen signum esse intelligit, nec ipse premitur servitute.*

63 *De doctr. Christ.* III.8.12.

64 See H. M. Féret, 'Sacramentum – Res dans la langue théologique de Saint Augustin', *Rev. des Sc. phil. et théol.* 29 (1940) 218–43.

65 See especially the studies by C. P. Mayer, *Die Zeichen in der geistigen Entwicklung und in der Theologie des jungen Augustinus* (Cassiciacum, 24/1. Würzburg, 1969) and *Die Zeichen in der geistigen Entwicklung und in der Theologie Augustinus*: II. Teil: *Die antimanichäische Epoche* (Cassiciacum, 24/2. Würzburg, 1974).

device to define a premature closure of biblical discourse, short of the new realm of meaning it would enter in the light of the Incarnation. We do not for our purposes need to follow him into his subtle discussion of the special role of the signs of the Old dispensation, or of the historical destiny of the Jews.[66]

But the Jews are, of course, by no means the only people who enclosed themselves in a circumscribed, restricted world of meanings. We are all capable of failing or refusing to look beyond the things of our immediate experience or beyond the direct literal meaning of signs to what may lie beyond. What Augustine has to say about the way that gentiles are subject to a 'servitude' to signs is therefore of considerable interest. They were subject to a different class of signs: and these bring us to considering not the *facta* recorded in the scriptures, but things in the world of creatures.

The Jews, Augustine said, had been subject to 'useful' signs instituted by God for their good; if it was 'carnal servitude' for them to stick to these when that which they were intended to signify had come to pass, 'how much worse is it to take the signs of useless things for the things themselves!'[67] The gentile counterpart of Jewish blindness is idolatry, that is to say, subjection to what Augustine called 'useless signs'. Unlike the Jews, the gentiles worshipped man-made images (*simulacra manufacta*).[68] As Augustine will concede, some pagans, 'those

66 On this see now P. Fredriksen, 'Excaecati Occulta Justitia Dei: Augustine on Jews and Judaism', *JECS* 3 (1995) 299–324.

67 *De doctr. Christ.* III.7.11: *Si ergo signum utiliter institutum pro ipsa re sequi, cui significandae institutum est, carnalis est servitus; quanto magis inutilium rerum signa instituta pro rebus accipere?*

68 *De doctr. Christ.* III.6.11. The account of idolatry in 6.11–9.13 is more fully developed in *Enarr. in Ps.* 113.ii.3–5 (on which see A. Mandouze, 'Saint Augustin et la religion romaine', *RechAug* 1 (1958) 187–223, at 207–10); *Sermo* Mainz 13.8–9; 62.17–24, 35 (ed. F. Dolbeau, *REAug* 39 (1993) 97–106 at 101–02; *RechAug* 26 (1992) 90–141, at 103–07; 117). Cf. also *Enarr. in Ps.* 96.11–12; *De mor.* I.34.75 (on which see below, at n. 85); *C. Faust.* XIV.12. The same argument recurs in different terminology in *Ep.* 102.iii.19.

of more refined religion',[69] will protest: they do not worship
the visible images; they bow in homage before them in the
gesture of *adoratio* – the gesture also used to honour the
emperor. But what they worship is not the material object, but
that of which it is a sign: its *numen*, the divinity it represents.[70]
In polemical contexts Augustine liked to impale his pagan
opponents on the horns of a dilemma: either they demean
themselves by worshipping a lifeless, material, image, in
which case they worship something lower in the order of
nature than they are themselves; or, if they are more sophisticated and worship something of which the image is a sign, they
worship something demonic.[71] Whereas the Jew fails through
remaining captive to the sign, the idolater fails either way:
whether he worships the sign itself, or that which it signifies.

The real interest of Augustine's treatment of the pagan's
subjection to idols, however, is that it provides a key to what
he thought about a much more general and fundamental
enclosure within a world of things which can and should be
taken as signs. There is a striking and exact parallel between
Augustine's treatment of the significance of idols, and of
material things in general. Consider what he has to say about
idols (*simulacra*)[72] in a harangue addressed to an imagined
pagan who claims to be worshipping a god: we can put his god
to the question, says Augustine; not in a question asked aloud,
but by looking at its form. 'By my looking I am interrogating
the form – *species* – and the matter of that wooden thing;
. . . to all my interrogation that which you say is a god
answers, without voice, but more truly than you do in words:

---

69 *Enarr. in Ps.* 113.ii.4: *purgatioris . . . religionis.*

70 Augustine often uses *colere* and *adorare* convertibly; but when he
makes the distinction, his formal usage is: *adoratio* is what is performed
before the *simulacrum* of the divinity, of whose *numen* it is a sign and which
is the object which is worshipped (*colitur*). See e.g. *Enarr. in Ps.* 113.ii.3–5
and *Sermo Mainz* 13.8; 62.17; 35; *Sermo* 62.6.10.

71 See n. 68, above. Cf. *De ciu. Dei* VI.10.

72 *Enarr. in Ps.* 135.3: *simulacra quae Graece appellantur idola . . .*

it is wood'.[73] Any reader of the *Confessions* will immediately recognise here an inverted echo of the famous chapter in which Augustine puts to the question the created universe, the things around him: 'I asked the sea, the deeps, the living creatures that creep, and they responded: "We are not your God, look beyond us" '; and so on. 'And with a great voice they cried out: "He made us" (Ps. 99:3). My question was the attention I gave to them, and their response was their *species*.'[74] Created things speak of their maker: but only to those who can hear, indeed only when they are put to the question, and by an interrogator who has the power of judgement. Reading creatures as signs requires, as do the signs of the Old Testament, the right kind of reader, readers with the right semiotic intention.

In the next paragraph Augustine makes this explicit: 'created things do not answer those who question them if the power to judge is lost . . . the created order speaks to all, but is understood only by those who hear its outward voice and compare it with the truth within themselves',[75] that is to say, by those who are taught by Christ, the Interior Teacher. The language of the *Confessions*, non-technical as it is, makes use of the linguistic model which Augustine had carefully elaborated in his *De doctrina Christiana* not long before writing the *Confessions*. Although Augustine does not say created things are signs of their creator, here, or so far as I know elsewhere, the relationships he envisages evidently conform to those in a

---

73 *Sermo Mainz* 13.4: *Speciem ligni illius atque materiam interrogat aspectus meus . . . respondet se mihi lignum esse, quod tu dicis deum, sine voce sua, fidelior tamen quam vox tua.*

74 *Conf.* X.6.9: *interrogatio mea intentio mea et responsio eorum species eorum.* (In the translation by Henry Chadwick; I have left the last word – translated by Chadwick as 'beauty' – in the original, to indicate not only the greater richness of its meaning in Latin, but its affinity with the sense it bears in the previous passage. On the same lines, cf. *Enarr. in Ps.* 144.13–14; *Sermo* 241.2.2, where *pulcritudo* takes the place of *species*).

75 *Conf.* X.6.10.

semantic situation as he has represented them in the classic discussion of the *De doctrina Christiana*.[76] A sign, for Augustine, is something that stands for something to somebody; meaning is a triadic relation between a subject, the thing which is a sign (most typically, but not necessarily, a word), and the object it refers to. This clearly holds here, the relationship between the interrogator, the creatures put to the question, and the Creator. This triadic relation would not, by itself, justify us in assimilating this situation to that which we have in discourse; it could be analogous, for instance, to a doctor diagnosing an illness from a symptom. It would be eccentric to say that the spots signifying measles constitute a language understood by the doctor. But Augustine has invited us to make the assimilation to language, asking us to hear creatures speak and likening the order and harmony of God's creatures to that of a 'very beautiful poem', its beauty conferred on it by the divine rhetoric securing a proper disposition of components.[77] If we accept his invitation, we must note that it is a peculiar discourse he is asking us to participate in: it is somewhat repetitive, indeed only a single statement is made by creatures over and over again: 'He made us'.

It is tempting to take the easy refuge of saying that such a puzzle arises from taking too literally a fine image Augustine uses with great literary skill and with characteristically persuasive rhetoric. That he is doing this is true; but the temptation to leave it at this should, nevertheless, be resisted if we are to take the measure of the way Augustine saw his world. The theory of signs and meanings he elaborated in his *De doctrina Christiana* and the principles of scriptural hermeneutics elaborated there with its aid spills over into something like a general theory of understanding: a hermeneutics of human

76 Expounded in full in my papers referred to in n. 1, and below, Chapters 3 and 4.

77 *De civ. Dei* XI.18: *eloquentia rerum*.

experience.[78] The triadic pattern of subject–sign–signified is rather more than a mere rhetorical device for Augustine; it is a recurrent and fundamental pattern of his thinking; and so is, along with this triadic pattern, the idea of 'captivity' or 'servitude' to the sign: that is, our inability or unwillingness to go beyond and see behind what is immediately given; to seek meaning. This is something like a structural principle of his mature thought. What I am suggesting is that habits of reading the biblical text had profound repercussions on the way Augustine read his world.

Intention and the quest for meaning

The ability to read God's deeds in the Old Testament as His speech (*eloquentia divina*), and the ability to read God's creatures in the world as telling of their Creator (*eloquentia rerum*), both require the right disposition or intention as Augustine would say. The disposition to see things as signs, with a meaning beyond their obvious, immediate appearances is an intention to 'put them to the question'. Meaning is not obvious to us; our understanding is clouded. Fallen human beings as we are, we are permanently liable to failing to communicate and failing to be communicated with. In this life we are denied the transparency of mutual understanding which would allow direct communication between us and other minds.[79] Adam's sin has ruptured the primal community

78 Cf. the distinction made between 'macro-' and 'micro-hermeneutics' by W. Jeanrond, *Theological hermeneutics* (London, 1991) 3–9, the former being concerned with 'interpretation of the universe'.

79 For fuller accounts see my paper, 'Signs, communication and communities' (above, n. 1; Chapter 4 below), especially at notes 10–12, where further references are given; see also D. Dawson, 'Sign theory, allegorical reading and the motions of the soul in *De doctrina Christiana*', in the same collection, 123–41. See also C. Harrison, *Beauty and revelation in the thought of St Augustine* (Oxford, 1992) 59–67. The theme, especially in relation to the problems of body and soul, has been most recently laboured by C. Ando, 'Augustine on language', *REAug* 40 (1994) 45–78.

in which communication would have been effortless; now, in our sinful state, we need words and other signs. Without communication there can be no community. Our fallen communities are founded on the imperfect medium of language: 'I am saddened', Augustine wrote, 'that my words cannot suffice for my heart . . . Understanding flashes like lightning through the mind; but speech is slow and sluggish, and hopelessly inadequate . . .'[80] Although, therefore, the whole purpose of speech is to communicate, it is doomed to be an imperfect vehicle of meaning, always opening up a 'communication gap' between speaker and hearer. The sign always intrudes between them, as it intrudes between themselves and that which they speak about or wish to know about.[81] Hence the radical ambivalence of signs, their ability to conceal no less than to reveal. Meaning has often to be striven, even struggled for.

In a later work Augustine considers what happens when we do this.[82] What we search for, he answers, is an understanding of the opaque sign which will both disclose its meaning and enable us to communicate with others. The search for meaning is a quest for transcendence – transcendence of the self imprisoned among opaque signs, isolated from the linguistic community no less than from the realm of meanings accessible to it. In discovering the meaning of signs we discover a shared world of reference and in so doing are integrated into our linguistic community. The two things are, at bottom, identical: integration in the linguistic community *is* discovery of meaning, and the search for meaning heals ruptures in the

---

80 *De cat. rud.* 2.3: *Contristor linguam meam cordi meo non potuisse sufficere . . . intellectus quasi rapida coruscatione perfundit animum; illa autem locutio tarda et longa est, longeque dissimilis . . .*

81 See Rist, *Augustine* (see above, n. 1) 29–36, especially 32.

82 *De Trin.* X.1.2. For more detailed analysis, see my paper, 'Signs, communication and communities' (above, n. 1; below, Chapter 4, p. 105ff). On this passage see especially G. P. O'Daly, *Augustine's philosophy of mind* (London, 1987) 209.

linguistic community. Discovery of meaning frees us from captivity to the sign, and incorporates us in what we might call a textual, or an interpretative, community.

What, in the end, matters to Augustine is intention. It is intention that directs the will to understand and to communicate, and thereby determines the interpretative community to which one belongs. Nowhere is this clearer than in the way Augustine treats magic and cognate superstitious practices.[83] These practices rest on 'pacts about certain meanings agreed with demons by contract'.[84] These practices presuppose a shared semantic system and communication within a community of shared intentions. The magical rituals constitute the language shared by the magician and the demons. Augustine envisages this community as brought into being through evil men, seeking their own, selfish and 'private' ends, being assisted by demonic powers similarly intent on their own, 'private', glorification. The community sharing a symbolic system is brought into being by the identity of intentions. Significantly, Augustine will allow that superstitious practices are often carried out even by those 'who profess the name of Christians'; 'it is hardly surprising in so vast a multitude of people', he argued, that many will have betrayed their baptismal vows to renounce this world, and will nevertheless have succumbed to its ways. But he is quite clear about the gulf between such back-sliders and people who really have identified themselves with the society of demons.[85] They lack the semantic intention that would unite them into the demonic society. They deploy the signs without effectively communicating by their means.

83 See Chapter 5 below.

84 *De doctr. Christ.* II.20.30: *pacta quaedam significationum cum daemonibus placita atque foederata.*

85 *De mor.* I.34.75. Augustine is writing here especially about Christians 'adoring' pictures or participating in traditional funeral practices and banquets. The practice is described in the *Consultationes Apollonii et Zacchaei* (ed. J. L. Feiertag, *Sources chrétiennes* 401–02. Paris, 1994) I.28.

Interpretative communities

We are now in a position to return to the point I mentioned a while ago that we would need to consider: Augustine's insistence that a text requires the right kind of reader to understand it. A text must have its readers, and readers form interpretative communities. Augustine takes his principle that communities are formed by communication very seriously:

> That which is rational in us, that is to say, that which uses reason, and makes or follows what is reasonable, has imposed words, that is to say, certain meaningful sounds, upon things. It has done this because it draws us into association by a kind of natural bond with those with whom we share rationality; and men could not be solidly associated with one another unless they could talk to each other and by doing so share, as it were, what is in their minds and their thoughts. For as we cannot feel one another's minds, they can nevertheless be joined together by shared meanings, as if through an interpreter.[86]

Speech is the very condition of rational association, the 'interpreter' between minds which, without it, would remain opaque to each other; and the written text, as Augustine goes on to state in the immediate sequel, is the means whereby the absent can be drawn into the group communicating by means of speech. One will, obviously, have to know the language in which a text is written; that is to say, one will have to belong to what we might call a primary linguistic community, of

---

86 *De ord.* II.12.35: *Namque illud quod in nobis est rationale, id est, quod ratione utitur, et rationabilia vel facit vel sequitur, quia naturali quodam vinculo in eorum societate adstringebatur, cum quibus illi erat ratio ipsa communis, nec homini homo firmissime sociari posset, nisi colloquerentur, atque ita sibi mentes suas cogitationesque quasi refunderent, vidit esse imponenda rebus vocabula, id est significantes sonos, ut quoniam sentire animos suos non poterant, ad eos sibi copulandos sensu quasi interprete uterentur.*

English-speakers, or Latin–speakers, or whatever. But one will have to belong to a further, perhaps a secondary linguistic, or let us say textual, or even interpretative, community, or to more than one. We can fail to understand the Bible's figurative language, the meaning of its 'transferred signs', Augustine says, both through ignorance of its language and through ignorance of the realities it signifies.[87] How can we appreciate the scriptural symbolism of the serpent, Augustine asks, if we don't know what snakes really are like?[88] Hence the importance he attaches – even if only at a minimal level – to the secular discourses of the natural sciences, of history and geography and so forth, for understanding the biblical discourse. There is, however, a further dimension of meaning, which we have already touched on, peculiar to the understanding of the scriptures, more precisely, of the Old Testament. For it is this that is taken up into a new realm of meaning in the light of the Incarnation;[89] and it is this meaning that Christian freedom has made accessible to those liberated from subjection to the signs of the Old Testament 'by raising them, through interpreting the signs to which they were subject, to the things of which those signs were the signs'.[90] In the language I have – anachronistically – adopted, the Christian community is an interpretative community, with its own special mode of access to the figurative meanings of the Old Testament. There will, necessarily, be a whole hierarchy of interpretative communities, from the most inclusive to the more specific: say from those who understand the language of the text, to those who understand it in a particular way. A Christian understanding of a canonical text is always one

87 *De doctr. Christ.* II.16.23.
88 *De doctr. Christ.* II.16.24. See on this Irvine, *The making*, 262–65; 'Typological meaning depends on a knowledge of sacred history regulated by a code that establishes correspondences between events' (262).
89 *De doctr. Christ.* III.5.9–6.10. Cf. above, n. 61.
90 *De doctr. Christ.* III.8.12.

which involves both a certain latitude, which is, in other
words, radically pluralistic, while, at the same time, involving
some limits to pluralism.[91]

Augustine made extensive use of his model of what is
involved in understanding the figurative sense of the scriptures; and, if my suggestion is accepted, he used the same
model to represent the relationships between human creatures, their world and their creator. It would seem to follow
that in this case, too, those who are able to see the world of
creatures as pointing beyond themselves to a Creator form an
interpretative community; a community wider than the Christian community, for they share an attitude towards the world,
a cosmic text, not the more restricted text of the Bible.
Augustine does not explore the nature of this larger community. I suppose, if we try to define it on his behalf, in line with
the pointers he gives us, it would be the community of human
beings who act in line with their true rational nature, made in
the image of God, 'those who hear its outward voice and
compare it with the truth within themselves'.[92] Such a
community will be more comprehensive than the Jewish and
the Christian communities, defined by their alternative hermeneutical stance towards the biblical text. It will include
these, but along with them it will also include all who share a
hermeneutic stance towards the world such that they can
perceive its transcendence and are freed from living in a closed
world of creatures. If this seems to be stretching the schemat-
ism of Augustine's theory of signs unduly, I would plead that
it is stretching it in a very authentically Augustinian direction.
For as I have argued, Augustine is serious, even if somewhat
metaphorical, in insisting that the world of creatures is to be
taken as text.

In the next chapter I shall suggest that this model of text and

---

91 On the unity of scripture and the pluralism in the Christian community, see Williams, 'The literal sense' (see above, n. 4).

92 *Conf.* X.6.10 (see above, n. 75).

world underwent a profound shift in the two hundred years after Augustine: so profound that we can speak of the replacement of a Late Antique by a medieval world view.

Additional note: Exegesis, interpretation, tradition and textual communities

We have noted (above, n. 51) a distinction suggested by Augustine between two approaches to a text. I quote the passage again here:

> The first [type of enquiry about a text] concerns the truth of the matter in question. The second concerns the intention of the writer. It is one thing to enquire into the truth about the origin of the creation. It is another to ask what understanding of the words on the part of a reader and hearer was intended by Moses . . .

I labelled these two kinds of enquiry 'exegesis' and 'interpretation' respectively. Augustine's own practice in fact conforms to this distinction. He recognises an interpretative activity which is neither literal nor allegorical exegesis. Let me try to elucidate this.

His commentary on Genesis in Books XII and XIII of the *Confessions* was overtly allegorical, concerned rather to trace the itinerary of his restless heart to the 'peace of repose, the peace of the sabbath without an evening'[93] than to expound what was in the mind of the author. In the allegorical exposition he had undertaken here this is not anomalous. What seems more at variance with his professed hermeneutical theory is the range that his 'interpretation' encompasses even when he is pursuing a literal exegesis, as he says he is doing in the Literal Commentary on Genesis.[94] Books X and XII are avowedly digressions; but what is significant about the work

93 *Conf.* XIII.35.50: *pacem quietis, pacem sabbati, pacem sine vespera . . .*
94 *Retract.* II.24.1; *De Gen. ad litt.* I.1.2.

as a whole is how little the digressions seem to differ from the
substance. The whole commentary, especially Books I-VII,
reads like a string of digressions, more or less developed, held
together only by the sequence of the scriptural texts they are
strung on. This is precisely what gives the work its interest: we
can observe Augustine in the act of enquiry, raising questions,
debating the answers, leaving problems unresolved; he is in his
intellectual workshop.[95] It is not for what it tells us about
Augustine's views on the first three chapters of Genesis, but
for what it tells us about his ideas on human nature, on
sexuality, on the nature of the soul, and so forth, that we read
it. On no reckoning could this count as literal, or, for that
matter, even as typological exegesis of the first verses of
Genesis. But it is not allegory either.[96]

Augustine himself seems to have been aware of the difference between two activities which I noted above and labelled
'exegesis' and 'interpretation' respectively. Here he is concerned with discovering the truth about a number of things
related to the texts he is commenting on, rather than the truth
about what was meant by their author. Augustine might have
been expected to apply that distinction here; but he does not
do so, while insisting that he is interpreting the text in its literal

95 *Retract.* II.24 (51): *In quo opere plura quaesita quam inventa sunt, et
eorum quae inventa sunt, pauciora firmata, cetera vero ita posita velut adhuc
requirenda sint.* Cf. *De Gen. ad litt.* XII.1.1.

96 In the sense discussed by, for instance, P. Ricoeur, *Interpretation
theory. Discourse and the surplus of meaning* (Ft. Worth, 1976) 56: 'allegory
is a rhetorical procedure that can be eliminated once it has done its job'.
Augustine also distinguishes *ficta* such as parables and metaphors as a
separate category of symbolic expression which is neither false nor, literally,
true: *Q. Evang.* II.50.1. Compare the description of poetic discourse as
suspending the descriptive function of language, restoring participation and
manifesting rather than stating truth by P. Ricoeur, *Essays on biblical
interpretation*, ed. L. S. Mudge (London, 1981) 100–04. Could Augustine's
distinction perhaps be stated in terms of 'dialogical understanding' of a text?
Cf. D. LaCapra, *Rethinking intellectual history: texts, contexts, language*
(Ithaca, 1983) 23–71.

sense. His procedure, as his commentators have observed, is disconcerting;[97] but not because, as they suggest, he has in many places superimposed allegorical interpretation on literal exegesis, but because much of the time in this Commentary he is in fact engaged in an altogether different sort of enterprise, what I have called 'interpretation' as distinct from 'exegesis'.

What Augustine is doing here is more accurately described as interpreting his experience, or his world view, in the light of the scriptural text, rather than the scriptural text in the light of his experience. He is undertaking something very like the task described by Ricoeur: 'The hermeneutic task ... is to broaden the comprehension of the text on the side of doctrine, of practice, of meditation on the mysteries. And consequently it is to equate the understanding of meaning with a total interpretation of existence and of reality in the system of Christianity.'[98] In both, the reader is actively involved, the act of reading generating a tension between the world of the text and the world of the reader. Ricoeur does not make the distinction between 'exegesis' and 'interpretation' which I have foisted on to Augustine's hint of two distinct activities undertaken by the commentator on the Bible. Although the vocabulary was not, of course, available to Augustine, he was, as we have seen, feeling his way towards something not unlike such a distinction. If we adopt it now, it will enable us to state his apparent intention in this way: in 'exegesis', the text remains the focus of interest, whatever interpretative method is adopted to expound it. It determines the direction of intellectual effort and the object of the striving to understand. 'Interpretation' is less focused on the text; it can bring into play a much wider range of concepts, images, systems of ideas.

97 On Augustine's procedure in this work, see Solignac's Introduction to it, *loc. cit.* (above, n. 47) 1.35; for discussion of Augustine's procedure, see the whole section, 32–50.

98 Ricoeur, *Essays on biblical interpretation*, 53; see also the distinction made between 'macro-' and 'micro-hermeneutics' by Jeanrond, *Theological hermeneutics* (above, n. 78).

Exegesis remains confined within the framework of the discourse of the text, whereas interpretation may range more widely, even outside the kind of discourse determined by the nature of text being interpreted.

How can this distinction be stated in a more precise form? Stated in more general terms by anthropological writers, exegesis is confined by the limits of the culture characterised by the texts and practices which the exegete confronts; interpretation is undertaken from outside these limits: '[Exegesis], we can say, is the incessant commentary that a culture makes on its symbolism, its gestures, its practices, on all that constitutes it as a system in action. Exegesis proliferates from inside; it is a speech which nourishes the tradition of which it is a part, whereas interpretation emerges the moment there is an outside perspective, when some in a society begin to question, to criticize the tradition, to distance themselves with regard to the histories of the tribe.'[99] A similar distinction is made by James Barr, in terms of the homogeneity or heterogeneity of the interpretation: 'with interpretative methods such as typology and allegory a great deal depends on the nature of what we may call the "resultant" system. There are two systems or levels at work: the first is the text, the second is the system into which the interpretation runs out.'[100] 'Where an allegorizer by his interpretation finds a sense which belongs to quite a different world of thought, his results are heterogeneous from the text he is handling.'[101] Interpretation, taken in the sense I am distinguishing it here from 'exegesis', can come very close to (heterogeneous) allegorical exegesis, in that both take place outside the framework of discourse set by the text. But interpretation need not be allegorical, and usually

99 M. Detienne, 'Rethinking mythology', in *Between belief and transgression*, ed. M. Izard & P. Smith (Chicago, 1982) 43–52, at 48.

100 In his *Old and new in interpretation: a study of the Two Testaments* (London, 1966) 108. The whole chapter on Typology and Allegory (103–48) is the most illuminating discussion of this question I have come across.

101 *Ibid.*, 116.

takes a form very different from that of allegory, in any normal sense of the word; its relation to the text is not that of allegory to letter. For this reason it is preferable to distinguish what I have called 'interpretation' from allegorical exegesis. It is also more in line with Augustine's procedure in the *De Genesi ad litteram*, described by him as 'literal'; but in fact much more far-ranging, though not 'allegorical' in the normal sense.

Exegesis and interpretation, understood in something like this way, both assume and take place within a social group, a culture or a sub-culture; but the groups or cultures may be different in the two cases. Exegesis will always take place within the bounds of a textual community; that is to say, in groups 'organized around common understanding of a script'.[102] There will be a comparatively large group defined by acceptance of a text as in some way authoritative, the Bible, the Koran, and so forth; this large group will comprise a spectrum of smaller sub-groups, committed to particular interpretative traditions of that text current within them. The formation of a fixed and written scripture leads to the consequence that the 'continuing extra-scriptural tradition became in many ways basically exegetical: it might continue to have its own starting-points and its own content, but it already acknowledged as a matter of fact the now fixed scripture as an authority over itself'.[103] 'Why do you not submit yourself',

102 B. Stock, *Listening for the text: On the uses of the past* (Baltimore, 1990) 23 (where the groups are called 'microsocieties': implying a restriction of scale which I regard as arbitrary). Cf. also pp. 140–58. What is said in the text is not, of course, intended to suggest that exegesis can only be carried out by those who belong to the community in question, e.g. the Christian Church. Exegetes who do not belong put themselves temporarily into the position of believers, suspending disbelief. They would, of course, have no reason to 'interpret' a scriptural text in the sense of formulating their own world view or experience in its terms.

103 J. Barr, 'The Bible as a document of believing communities', in *Explorations in theology, 7: The scope and authority of the Bible* (London, 1980) 111–33, at 121.

Augustine asked a Manichaean opponent, 'to the authority of the gospels . . . warranted by the most certain continuity of transmission from the times of the apostles down to our own times?' They appeal to their own scripture, and disparage the Catholics' reliance on the authenticity of the apostolic writings; 'if you ask us how we know these writings to be the apostles', we shall briefly reply that we know them to be so just as you know your writings to be Mani's'.[104] To be a Christian, Augustine is saying, is to belong to the community which has given these writings their authority and continues to submit itself to it.

Augustine was sharply, and among ancient writers I think uniquely, insistent on the social construction of all meanings. Linguistic communities are constituted by shared understanding of a 'language' (I am for the present purpose using the word in a very wide and necessarily imprecise sense). Semantic activity exists for the sole purpose of communicating with others;[105] and meaningful communication is, for Augustine, the basic condition for human community: 'there could be no solid association between men unless they could communicate and unless they could thus share, as it were, their minds and their thoughts'.[106] Language bridges the gulf that has opened up between fallen human beings, and thus creates communi-

---

104 C. Faust. XXXII.19–22: *cur non potius evangelicae auctoritati . . . ab apostolorum temporibus usque ad nostra tempora per successiones certissimas commendatae, non te subdis . . .?* (19); . . . *Hic iam si quaeratis a nobis nos unde sciamus apostolorum esse istas litteras, breviter vobis respondemus, inde nos scire unde et vos scitis illas litteras esse Manichaei . . .* (21).

105 Thus *signa data* are defined as: *quae sibi quaeque viventia invicem dant ad demonstrandos, quantum possunt, motus animi sui, vel sensa aut intellecta quaelibet* – De doctr. Christ. II.2.3; the only reason for signifying, that is, for giving signs (*significandi, id est signi dandi*) is to bring forth (*ad depromendum*) what is going on in the mind of the sign-giver and to communicate it (*ad traiciendum*) to another's mind.

106 De ord. II.12.35: *nec homo homini firmissime sociari posset, nisi colloquerentur atque ita sibi mentes suas cogitationesque quasi refunderent.* Cf. above, n. 86.

ties. Particular languages create particular communities; and special languages within these create sub-communities, or sub-cultures. This is of special importance for Augustine in the discussion of textual communities. For as we have seen, the language of the scriptures often has meanings on two levels: the direct meaning of the words, and other realities which the words may be used to signify in the divine language which speaks with facts as well as with words. To understand the meaning of the words, what one needs is to understand the Latin language.[107] To perceive a *further* significance one needs more: to know what the thing is used in the scriptural context to signify. And to know this, is to belong to a further linguistic community, superimposed, so to speak, on the fundamental linguistic community of Latin-speakers; perhaps a linguistic community (a sub-culture?) of Latin-speakers whose minds are formed by the speech–habits of scriptural usage.

It is this textual community that Augustine has in mind when he comes to discuss what is involved in understanding (or failure to understand) *signa translata*.[108] To understand figurative signs, we must know not only the literal meaning of their names (what they primarily refer to); we must also be familiar with the further reference that scripture habitually ascribes to the primary referent of the word. Thus Augustine states the difference between the Jewish and the Christian communities essentially in hermeneutic terms: the Jews refused to understand the Old Testament in its 'figurative' sense, that is to say as interpreted in the New; and similarly, he defines magical practice and ritual in terms of communities sharing a language.[109] Traditions of interpretation generate communities; and interpretation is a social construction of meaning related to a text.

The historical sense of a scriptural text is its direct extra-

107 *De doctr. Christ.* II.11.16.
108 *De doctr. Christ.* II.16.23.
109 See further Chapter 5 below.

linguistic referent; the interpretative tradition(s) provide 'what amounts to a series of semiotic systems which allow meanings to be generated outside the primary (historical) semiotic system'; and as Hans Georg Gadamer observes, 'understanding is not so much an action of one's own subjectivity' as 'the placing of oneself within a process of tradition, in which past and present are constantly fused'.[110] Hence it follows that interpretations of texts are not entirely determined by individual choices. 'Choice is not unconditioned; we do not choose the model of God as shepherd over that of God as poultry keeper or cattleman at random.'[111] Texts have authority within a community, as understood in terms of the traditions that have formed and sustained that community. The texts authoritative within a community are not 'texts–in–themselves', severed from the community's experience; they come laden with the weight, and authority, of a tradition of experience and interpretation. The scriptures themselves are the deposit of a long process of the formation and the revision of traditions;[112] their interpretation, similarly, is the product of cumulative, growing, albeit more diverse, traditions: 'Its [Christianity's] sacred texts are chronicles of experience, armouries of metaphor, and purveyors of an interpretative tradition. The sacred literature thus both records the experience of the past and provides the descriptive language by which any new experience may be interpreted.'[113] An individual's 'experience is interpreted by his sacred texts, his

110 A. C. Thiselton, *New horizons in Hermeneutics* (London, 1992) 144; the quotation from H. G. Gadamer's *Truth and method*, 258 is taken from Thiselton, 147.

111 J. Soskice, *Metaphor as religious language* (Oxford, 1985) 158. It is models on which God is represented that are under discussion here; the statement is, however, equally valid for the way biblical symbols are understood.

112 See on this much of the work of James Barr; especially his *The scope and authority of the Bible* and *Old and new in interpretation*.

113 Soskice, *Metaphor*, 160.

sacred texts are reinterpreted in his own experience, the whole is founded upon centuries of devotional practice . . .',[114] and, we might add, of exegesis and interpretation. The authority of the text will remain there, given, in all our reappraisals of the possibilities of meaning in it.[115]

114 *Ibid.*, 159.

115 The phrase 'reappraisal of the possibilities for meaning' is Barr's: see *Old and new in interpretation*, 185. See also Lamberton, *Homer the theologian*, 304, on interpretation as projection of meanings, and text as breaking down preconceived ideas: 'an essentially destructive process by which the meaning of the text (or of the spoken sentence) realizes itself in our consciousness by displacing and modifying our preconceptions'.

Chapter Two
WORLD AND TEXT IN ANCIENT CHRISTIANITY II: GREGORY THE GREAT[1]

From Augustine's world to Gregory's

It is hardly necessary to remark that some fundamental intellectual shift divided medieval Christianity from the Christianity of Late Antiquity; but to describe it is much harder. It has been characterised in many ways: in terms of intellectual impoverishment, of an epistemological crisis, of superstition replacing reason, and many more. In this chapter I shall suggest that one of the ways in which this shift might be described is in terms of the way Christians read their scriptures and the ways in which they read their world in relation to their reading of the scriptures. This is rather a convoluted statement, and it involves far too much 'reading'; in a moment I shall try to elucidate it. In my first lecture I took Augustine to represent – albeit in an unusually sophisticated and articulate shape – a Christian of around AD 400. Now I shall take Gregory the Great to represent his counterpart some 200 years later.

It is useful to bear in mind some immediately obvious and relevant differences which need not, however, be dwelt upon. First, that Augustine breathed the air of a mixed and varied intellectual culture and engaged in debate with educated

1 I have made considerable use in this lecture of my paper 'The Jew as a hermeneutic device: the inner life of a Gregorian *topos*', forthcoming in the proceedings of the Notre Dame Symposium on Gregory the Great, and wish to thank the Editor, John Cavadini, for his permission to do so.

people who did not share his religion or his world view. He
read Cicero, Virgil, Plotinus and Porphyry and other ancient
writers, Christian and non-Christian. Gregory read Augustine. As John Rist remarked in his fine recent study of
Augustine's thought, Augustine 'bequeathed himself . . . to
his Western successors . . . For all his foresight, Augustine
could not conceive of a Christian thinker being more or less
comfortable in Christendom.'[2] Gregory was comfortable in
the world he saw through his Christian eyes. Its intellectual
contours were shaped by ideas in great part derived from
Augustine. Of course, he too had read the works of some
other, mainly Latin Christian writers; but in all essentials it
was Augustine's conceptual structures that shaped the world
of his imagination.

Gregory was also 'comfortable' in his world in another,
though related, sense, which is even more important for our
purpose.[3] His world had become a Christian world in a
manner Augustine could not have imagined. Augustine's
society was still a complex fabric of intellectual and religious
traditions of great diversity. In his world the question that
haunted thoughtful Christians was 'what is a Christian?',
'what is it that distinguishes him from his non-Christian
fellows?' In Gregory's world the question had become redun-
dant; everyone, for practical purposes, was a Christian. Even
the excluded few – Jews, heretics, rustics labelled by bishops
as pagans – would be defined in religious terms, measured by
norms laid down by Christian clergy. Christianity could now
be taken for granted; there may still be some, Gregory
conceded, 'who perhaps do not carry the Christian name'; but
if there were such, they were marginal, and he was more

2 *Augustine. Ancient thought baptized* (Cambridge, 1994) 290; 291
(italics in original).

3 On this see my 'The sacred and the secular: from Augustine to Gregory
the Great', *JThS* n.s. 36 (1985) 84–96 (reprinted in *Sacred and secular*
(London, 1994) II).

interested in those who do bear the name, but are like the *iniqui* who 'deviate from righteousness by the wickedness of their works', who are Christians in name only, from outward conformity.[4]

Gregory's horizons were those of the Christian scriptures. His way of reading the scripture is radically monastic. 'It shows the perfectionism of the monastic ideal extended out onto the Church and to every human soul.'[5] Where in an earlier age the divide would have run between the Church and the unregenerate world outside it, for Gregory it ran between the less and the more perfect within the Church. For him, the Church had come to swallow up the world. He could think of *conversio* more easily as something undergone by the Christian soul on its way to perfection, than of a non-Christian to Christianity.[6] The complexity of Augustine's world had collapsed into simplicity. Compared with Augustine, Gregory could take for granted the settled contours of his spiritual landscape. Christianity had come to give definitive shape to a 'totalising discourse'. How to be a Christian, how to live the fullest Christian life: this was Gregory's central preoccupation in all his preaching; and this was the question into which the anxieties of his age had shaped themselves. Naturally, it helped to give Gregory's exegesis a predominantly moral direction.

---

4 *Mor.* XVIII.6.12: *impius namque pro infideli ponitur, id est a pietate religionis alienus; iniquus vero dicitur, qui pravitate operis ab aequitate discordat, vel qui fortasse christianae fidei nomen non portat.* Cf. XXVII.18.36–37; *Hom. in Ev.* II.29.4 and II.32.5 on Christians in name only.

5 E. A. Matter, *The voice of my beloved: the Song of Songs in Western medieval Christianity* (Philadelphia, 1990) 96. I have argued that this way of reading was already established in ascetic circles in the time of Cassian and Salvian; see my *The end of ancient Christianity* (Cambridge, 1990) 165–70.

6 *Hom. in Hiez.* I.10.9–11. See also C. Straw, *Gregory the Great. Perfection in imperfection* (Berkeley, 1988) 194–235, and C. Dagens, *Saint Grégoire le Grand. Culture et expérience chrétiennes* (Paris, 1977) 247–346.

Gregory's scriptural hermeneutics and Augustine's

Being a man much less inclined than was Augustine to analyse troubling intellectual problems, Gregory took no interest in theoretical discussion of signification and meaning. He held Augustine in high regard; but it was Augustine's exegetical practice rather than his theory that he followed, and Augustine's practice was often, as I noted in my first chapter, far less rigorous than the hermeneutic theory that he formulated would have allowed. (In the sequel, I shall often use the shorthand 'Augustine's allegorical interpretation' (or exegesis) to refer to those of his figurative interpretations of biblical texts which came to predominate in his writings, that is to say those which would be sanctioned by his theoretical discussion and which he came, increasingly, to prefer to unrestrained allegorising. See Chapter 1, pp. 8–11) Gregory had none of the hesitations that led Augustine, as we have seen, to distrust allegory and to restrict its practice more and more as he thought out the nature of text and meaning. Quite the contrary: if Augustine's hermeneutic is based on a steady retreat from allegory, Gregory's was based from start to finish on its ready availability.[7] With Gregory we are in a different world of exegesis. The difference is tantalisingly hard to describe, for in practice Gregory's exegeses are so often like Augustine's.[8] But we must attempt to describe the difference. Though very elusive in appearance, it will turn out to be actually quite fundamental.

7 On Gregory's terminology, see Matter, *The voice of my beloved*, 55, 94–95. I shall use 'allegorical' in the wide sense to include Gregory's 'moral' or 'tropological' sense, and equivalent to 'spiritual'.

8 For a thorough charting of Gregory's debt to Augustinian exegesis in one set of Homilies, see D. Eisenhofer, 'Augustinus in den Evangelien–Homilien Gregors des Grossen. Ein Beitrag zur Erforschung der literarischen Quellen Gregors des Grossen', in *Festgabe für Alois Knöpfler*, hrg. H. M. Geitl & D. G. Pfeilschrifter (Freiburg, 1917) 56–66. For a more general discussion, see V. Recchia, 'La memoria di Agostino nella esegesi biblica di San Gregorio Magno', *Augustinianum* 25 (1985) 405–34.

Let me begin with the more apparent differences. First, there is Gregory's marked preference for allegorical exposition,[9] contrasting with Augustine's growing distrust of it. I need not dwell too much on this. It quickly becomes apparent to anyone who dips into any collection of his homilies. Take, for example, Gregory's exegesis of chapter 14 in the first Book of Kings. Turning aside from the bloody battle with the Philistines which is the subject of the narrative he is commenting on, he quickly rises into the thinner air of his chosen theme: 'because we are describing the course of a spiritual battle, we must continue what has gone before in what is to follow'.[10] And continuing what has gone before is just what Gregory goes on to do, giving up the pretence of following the sequence of the text; it is no longer the text, but the dynamic of expounding his chosen subject that sets the hermeneutical framework. He is not often so explicit as this; but any reader of, for instance, his *Moralia*, will be familiar with those sustained treatises on themes near to his heart which Gregory will every now and then indulge in. Gregory's commentary has its own rich and complex logic; but it is not that of the modern, or indeed the ancient, scripture-commentator. With a freedom unrestrained by the text he can assemble biblical texts to create 'carefully crafted passages of teaching'.[11] Such passages, very frequent in his homilies, are held together not by an interest in the text, but by the overall theme the texts are assembled to support and to orchestrate. Whatever the exegetical cost, it is the continuity of the subject matter that

9 In common with most scholars, for example C. Dagens, *Saint Grégoire le Grand* (see above, n. 6, 233–46), I regard Gregory's distinction between literal (or 'historical') and allegorical as the fundamental one (see e.g. *Hom. in Ez.* I.9.30). I shall note the importance of the moral (or 'tropological') sense for Gregory, but shall not otherwise concern myself with the further divisions within the 'spiritual' sense.

10 *In Lib. I Reg.* V.153.

11 See G. Zinn, in the forthcoming Notre Dame Symposium, referred to above, n. 1.

dominates the sequence of the exposition. The treatise may have its origin in the text; but once it takes off from that diving board, the periodic returns to the text, under the guise, of course, of 'figurative' exposition (I refrain, for the present purpose, from the finer distinctions Gregory makes between the different sorts of figurative exposition), are simply conventional conformity with the *genre*. This is not without good rhetorical warrant and precedent, but it is exegetical freewheeling, all the same. And it is only on the rarest of occasions that Gregory will acknowledge that what he is doing is to indulge in a digression – as he does in the notorious case of the thirty fourth of his Homilies on the Gospels. There he was expounding the lost-and-found stories of Luke 15:1–10. Halfway through a rather fine sermon on repentance, a sermon well-anchored in his text, he will break off, with rather less than minimal support in his text, to expound the hierarchies of angels and their ministries, only to catch himself to admit, nine chapters later, just before the final vignette of the little story about penitence with which the sermon ends, that he has digressed.[12] Gregory's homiletic exposition can, and sometimes does, follow a path in its flight that manages to combine the logic of his text with that of his own thought; but the failure of the two to coincide must be so familiar to all readers of Gregory's homilies that I will refrain from mutiplying examples.

Reading his exegesis, the modern reader is apt to get the impression that his practice often suggests that he came quite close to believing that the letter really killeth; or, if it doesn't quite kill, that it at least induces a tedium which can only be lightened by hurrying over it as quickly as possible, and getting on with the much more serious business of the spirit.[13]

12 *Hom. in Ev.* II.34.1–5, mainly on repentance; 6–14: angels and the celestial hierarchy; 15–17: apology and return to God's mercy; 18: Maximian's story of Victorinus's penitence.

13 E.g. *Hom. in Ev.* II.40.2; *ibid.*, 3. Cf. *Mor.* XX.27.56, and, of course, the many places where he does this without saying so.

For Gregory the spirit listed inexorably in the direction of tropology. The *res gesta* generally signified a *gerendum*.[14] His primary interest is in the moral sense, that which teaches us how to act and conduct ourselves in the sight of God. The life of prayer, contemplation, self-denial and charity are the core of the message that the scriptures should convey to the Christian liberated from captivity to its letter.

The scripture, Gregory said, transcends all other knowledge (*scientiam atque doctrinam*); 'it calls all to our heavenly *patria*, it converts the hearts of its readers from earthly desires to embracing the higher good; by its more obscure sayings it exercises the minds of the stronger, by plain speech it pleases the weaker . . . in a certain sense, it grows with its reader'.[15] 'Openly, it provides food for the weakest, in secret it provides the means to raise the minds of the strongest to admiration'; it is like the river which is both shallow and deep, so that the lamb is not out of its depth and the elephant may swim.[16] People who, as Gregory said in one of his sermons, 'know how to draw many thoughts from a few words', will find in the text what they need.[17] It should be expounded to each according to his need and his capacity: the good preacher, Gregory says, will expound some things 'stooping to the level of the simplest (*minimis*), whereas others they will expound contemplating the highest things'.[18] Moral exposition is for all, but he must never forget the needs of the contemplative life: 'allegory', Gregory wrote, 'is a kind of pulley (*machina*) which enables a soul separated from God by a vast distance (*longe a Deo positae*) to be lifted up to God'.[19]

14 *Hom. in Ev.* II.21.2; cf. *Mor.* XIX.20.29: *ueraciter factum . . . significaret . . . ueraciter faciendum.*

15 *Hom. in Ez.* I.7.8: *Divina eloquia cum legente crescunt.*

16 *Ad Leandr.* 4.

17 *Hom. in Ev.* II.39.1: *ex paucis multa cogitare.*

18 *Mor.* V.11.24; XX.2.4; XXX.3.11–14; *Reg. Past.* III.

19 *Exp. in Cant.* 2; cf. 4; *Ad Leandr.* 2: *per contemplationis ascensum . . .*

Gregory's homiletic aims and his public

This is what the main bulk of his comments is about, and for which he is apt to neglect or to play down literal exposition of the text. The text becomes a storehouse of pegs on to which he hangs often quite extended treatises,[20] mostly concerned with moral and spiritual matters. The modern reader may yearn for the captivity to the letter from which Gregory felt himself delivered;[21] but we shall do better to try to follow him in his flight. He makes no secret of his destination: 'those who seek the purity of the contemplative life are to be shown not the ordinary things about the sacred scripture (*non communia de sacro eloquio*), but rather the higher and more sublime things, so that the more they are delighted by the superior goods (*nobiliora*) they hear about, the more ardently they might raise themselves to the heights by seeing'.[22] The text is a springboard for the contemplative, a flight from hearing to seeing.

The circumstances of much of his preaching are likely to have contributed something to bring this about. The greater part of Gregory's preaching was in fact addressed to a mixed public in which clergy or monks predominated, no doubt often including some lay-people, but a restricted group. Many of the homilies were addressed to a 'shifting diversity of listeners in a small group', some of whom were evidently monks, some clergy, some – like Gregory himself – in positions of high ecclesiastical authority, others on the fringes of ecclesiastical office, as assistants, 'helpers' of various kinds.[23] Gregory's homilies were delivered for the most part

20 See above, n. 11.

21 Even if he does not go quite as far as does F. H. Dudden, *Gregory the Great* (London, 1905) 1, 194–95.

22 *In I Lib. Reg.* III.124.

23 See A. de Vogüé, 'Les vues de Grégoire le Grand sur la vie religieuse dans son Commentaire des Rois', *StMon* 20 (1978) 17–63 (= 'The views of St Gregory the Great on the religious life in Commentary on the Book of Kings', *Cistercian studies* (1982) 40–64 and 212–32); and, especially, the characteristically thorough investigation by P. Meyvaert, 'The date of

to an ecclesiastical elite, a group of *rectores* or *praedicatores*, as Gregory would have called them, that is to say, to people who would be actually doing the preaching to others; as if he were teaching the teachers, as Augustine had been doing in works like the *De doctrina Christiana* or *De catechizandis rudibus*, rather than teaching the class, as Augustine had been in most of his preaching.

Both for Augustine and for Gregory, the final exegetical norm is the love that unites the interpretative community constituted by its understanding of the text. Building up the faithful community in love is the ultimate purpose of expounding the scriptures.[24] Gregory's exegetical norm is also communally conceived; but in a very different manner from Augustine's. The notion that the scriptures' spiritual sense feeds the contemplative life was, of course, well established long before Gregory. Gregory certainly shared this view, though he is unlikely, I think, to have wanted to go as far as did some earlier Christian writers towards actually asserting that a spiritual understanding of the scriptures actually *was* the contemplative life.[25] But what I want to draw attention to here is not so much Gregory's view on the purpose of scriptural understanding, as on its distribution in the Church. The people whom he is very often addressing, the class of *rectores* or *praedicatores*, are told how the scriptures are to be expounded to others, notably in their allegorical sense and generally to contemplatives, or would-be contemplatives. The

Gregory the Great's Commentaries on the Canticle of Canticles and on I Kings', *Sacris erudiri* 23 (1978–79) 191–216. Gregory's correspondence provides examples of a wide range of such officials. The phrase cited in the text, referring to the Commentary on I Kings, is quoted from Meyvaert, 'The date', 204–05.

24 Gregory, e.g. *Hom. in Ez.* I.10.4: *[verba Dei] ad hoc enim intelligenda sunt ut et nobis prosint et intentione spiritali aliis conferantur*; cf. *ibid.*, 14. For Augustine, see Chapter 1, n. 41, above.

25 I have argued that this was the case in John Cassian's *Conferences*; cf. my *The End of Ancient Christianity* (Cambridge, 1990) 184–89.

point deserves some emphasis, because there is a curious hierarchical consciousness about Gregory's hermeneutics which stems from his distinction of 'orders' within the Church. His distinction of three 'orders' in the Church is well known: they are the order of the rectors or preachers, of the continent, that is to say what we might call the professional religious, and the married. His language is fluid, and the terms tend to melt into each other, but the three *ordines* define the social structure of the Church, as of a society he does not distinguish from the Church.[26] What is less well known than this three-fold social or ecclesiastical hierarchy is a further subdivision Gregory introduced into the highest order, that of the *rectores* or *praedicatores*. Thus, for instance, expounding the 'gang of prophets' (I Kings 10:5–6), he asks:[27]

> Who are these prophets but the great preachers of the holy Church? For the ministry of prophets is to reveal what is hidden and to foretell what is to come. Teachers (*doctores*) of the holy Church, when they bring the hidden meanings of the scripture to general knowledge (*dum occultos scripturarum sensus ad communem scientiam trahunt*), lay open unknown secret depths; when they speak of the eternal joys, they reveal what is to come.

The Church's 'preachers' are equated with Israel's prophets; they have to come down to us from the heights in order to show us the way to the ascent of the mountain of God. Moreover, Gregory is very insistent on a further class sub-

26 On the *tres fidelium ordines*: e.g. *Hom. in Ez.* 2.4 (*praedicantium, continentium, coniugum*). On the *ordines* see G. Folliet, 'Les trois catégories de chrétiens', *Année théologique augustinienne* 14 (1954) 81–96. Cf. also my 'Gregory the Great on kings: rulers and preachers in the *Commentary on I Kings*', in *The Church and sovereignty*, ed. Diana Wood (Essays in honour of Michael Wilks, Studies in Church History, *Subsidia* 9, Oxford, 1991) 7–21 (reprinted in *Sacred and secular*, VIII), Additional Note on the Three Orders in the Church (20–21).

27 *In I Lib. Reg.* IV.173.

division, which he details in a puzzling passage: 'For there are three degrees of perfection', he goes on to tell us, within the *ordo* of *rectores*: on the lowest level is the *pastor*'s whose perfection consists in his obedience to his superiors (*praelatis*). On the next level, the *pastor* collaborates with his superiors. On the highest level, he matches his exalted position (*sublimitatem dignitatis*) by the splendour of his conduct, 'when, endowed with heavenly virtue, that life and that teaching shine upon his subjects which may be seen, but is not to be disputed or judged by them'.[28] The subdivision is evidently intended to distinguish various levels in the ecclesiastical hierarchy lumped together under the general heading of *rectores*, subgroups distinguished by their functions, which are in turn related to their characteristic virtues. Each of these levels is tantalisingly further characterised: obedience at the lowest rung pertains to hearing; collaboration at the second rung pertains to association; and at the summit, preaching is the defining characteristic. By it (together with the shining example of his life when the preacher has made it to conform with his preaching) the teaching will shine forth to his subjects. With the preacher we pass from the realm of hearing to that of seeing: with his enlightening labour – subsuming, evidently, the labours of his helpers lower in the hierarchy – the function of the whole hierarchy which constitutes the *ordo* of the *rectores* is to enlighten the Church as a whole, their 'subjects', all potentially contemplatives.

Exposition was the function of the *praedicator*, the *doctor*, the *rector*; but contemplation was a different matter altogether. This is not hierarchically distributed, but sometimes given even to those on the lowest rung of the ecclesiastical ladder, the *ordo* of the married.[29] The charismata of contemplation and of scriptural exposition could not be assumed to coincide in the same persons. It seems as if Gregory's

---

28 *In I Lib. Reg.* IV.195.
29 *Hom. in Ez.* II.5.19 (cf. II.7.3).

exegetical procedure is devised within the framework of his hierarchical model of the Church's *ordines*. Exposition of the scriptures is conceived primarily as the job of the *rectores* and *praedicatores*. Its aim is to feed contemplation, which is not a monopoly of their class but the spiritual ideal for all. Exposition is the bridge between the 'orders' in the Church. The *rectores* are the 'front windows' through which the heavenly light enters the Church; the lowly, the insignificant, who yield themselves to the desire for heavenly wisdom are the 'side windows, the windows in the vestibule'.[30] The fact that most of Gregory's preaching is addressed to people whose job will be to raise the level of Christian living, even, perhaps, to the heights of contemplation, may well be a contributory reason for the predominance of its moral orientation and allegorical procedure.

Lack of any interest in the theoretical foundations of signification; absence of concern for rules to limit the scope of acceptable interpretation; predominance of allegorical rather than literal exegesis, and, within this preference, a marked propensity towards the moral sense; what else can we put a finger on to distinguish Gregory's exegetical inclinations from Augustine's? These inclinations converge to allow Gregory far more freedom in interpreting his text than a more literalistic bent or a concern for rules would have sanctioned; but exegetical freedom or control by textual constraints are matters of degree, and anyway, as I have said, Augustine could indulge in exegetical free-wheeling quite as uninhibited as Gregory's – despite what his theoretical reflections and his professed intent pointed to. Gregory's exegetical practice contrasts far more sharply with Augustine's theory than with his practice. I want to suggest that this contrast, and indeed the differences between their instinctive exegetical preferences, are rooted in a more fundamental difference of hermeneutic stance, of attitude towards text and interpretation.

30 *Hom. in Ez*. II.5.20.

Gregory differed from Augustine in what really interested him, what he was prepared to be serious about. For comparison, let us look at a famous exchange of letters between Jerome and Augustine. Jerome – clearly wishing to make amends after a recent and more typically rancorous outburst[31] – proposed to Augustine that they agree to play together 'in the field of scripture without hurting one another'. Augustine, in his reply, accepted Jerome's proposal; but, revealingly, he added the proviso: only in so far as the 'playing' was taken to mean carrying on friendly discussion; for what was at stake was no playing matter. 'I would rather deal with these things seriously than in sport.'[32] What really mattered to Augustine was what the text said, how it was to be understood, and Jerome's expertise, he hoped, would help him to unravel the difficulties. They both appreciated the force of textual constraint; the meaning of the scripture was not to be determined by a free play of the imagination, even if informed by true piety. Compare Gregory: his scriptures are not quite a playing-field, but the next best thing: a pleasant, cool, forest for his recreation: 'Whenever we enter it by discussing it with understanding (*intelligendo discutimus*), what else are we doing than entering its refreshing shade to shelter from the heat of this world? There, reading, we munch the green shoots of its thoughts; expounding them we ruminate.'[33] Gregory

31 Cf. J. N. D. Kelly, *Jerome* (London, 1975) 264, who aptly characterises Jerome in this exchange as 'morbidly suspicious and ready to take offence'.

32 Augustine, *Ep.* 82.2, in answer to Jerome's *Ep.* 139 (= 81). I have not had the opportunity to consult R. Hennings, *Der Briefwechsel zwischen Augustinus und Hieronymus und ihr Streit um den Kanon des Alten Testaments und die Auslegung von Gal. 2, 11–14* (Leiden, 1994).

33 *Hom. in Ez.* I.5.1: *Ibique uiridissimas sententiarum herbas legendo carpimus, tractando ruminamus.* Cf. *In Cant.* 5 the spiritual mountain to be climbed by the inner man is *umbrosus per allegorias.* In *Hom. in Ez.* I.9.1, however, Gregory says he is emerging from the forest of Ezechiel's obscurity into the open meadows where the going is easier.

wanders about at his ease in the refreshing shade of the
scripture understood, of course, spiritually. The world it
refers to is more real than that from which it provides a shelter.
Here he is at home, he knows his way about its familiar paths,
delighting in the flowers he can pick as he wanders freely
among them. The bouquet assembled is nourishment for the
contemplative. The focus of attention is not the text, but the
spiritual doctrine that can be hung onto it. What matters is the
lesson taught by the text, or rather the lesson the expositor can
make the text point to for the contemplative's benefit. Any
notion of textual restraint is very distant. Commenting, as it
happens, on the verse 'He said to me: Son of man, go to the
house of Israel and speak to them my words' (Ezech. 3:4),
Gregory considers the restraint (*frenum*) that the Lord
imposes on the prophet's speech. In expounding the scriptures
the preacher must not try to please his audience: if he does, he
utters his own words, not the Lord's, so seducing his hearers.
Whereas:

> if one seeks virtue through the words of the Lord, even if
> they are understood differently than by their author,
> provided that even in their new meaning they aim to build
> up charity, the words uttered are the Lord's: for through-
> out the whole of the sacred scriptures God speaks to us
> with this one end, that He may draw us to love of Him
> and of our neighbour.[34]

Remarkably, what began as an interpretation of divine
restraint on the prophet's speech, ends with freeing the
expositor of holy scripture from the restraint of the text. The
only restraint is charity.

The criterion of exposition is, quite simply, efficacy in
building up charity. Gregory could have found a good deal in
Augustine's writings that may have seemed to him to warrant
such a view. As we saw in the last chapter, Augustine also
adopted charity as an exegetical criterion; but in a manner

34 *Hom. in Ez.* I.10.14.

very different from Gregory's.[35] Augustine took charity as a formal criterion of exegesis. It defined the limits within which an interpretation must fall. Any interpretation that breaches the command of charity cannot be a correct understanding. Augustine was careful to go on to say that a particular exegesis may serve the law of charity, but may nevertheless be mistaken; not culpably, but all the same, arriving at the right destination by a wrong route. And habitual taking of the wrong route, he says, can be dangerous.[36] To understand the text, he insists, is to read it in accordance with its author's intention.

If we follow the distinction between the two different activities made by Augustine which I considered in Chapter 1 (pp. 35–39), what Gregory is doing is neither 'exegesis' nor even 'interpretation'. We may, with Gregory and Augustine and much of the patristic tradition, call it allegorical interpretation; but we must be very clear about the gulf that separates it from the kind of figurative sense that Augustine's theory of signification in the Bible would have allowed. It is as if Gregory were familiar with the referents of the scriptural symbols, and had merely to choose the appropriate signifiers among the endless possibilities offered to him by the scriptural text. Between the two worlds of sign and meaning Gregory moved with an ease which was entirely foreign to Augustine. We do not find him searching, like Augustine, in the dark, among obscure symbols which stand between him and the realities they point to, significations which they are only too apt to conceal rather than to reveal, meanings to be carefully unravelled, not manifest. Augustine's forest is altogether darker, its paths less familiar and exploration more laborious. The signs speak a language more perplexing, governed by rules to be established and learned, perhaps painfully. Captivity to the letter was altogether less immediate a threat to Gregory

35 See Chapter 1, pp. 17–18.
36 *De doctr. Christ.* I.36.40–41.

than it had been for Augustine. The letter serves to propel Gregory – and anyone he expounds it to – into the realm of the spirit.

Gregory could read his world *through* the Bible with an ease Augustine could not have dreamed of. The significations of the text that Augustine had to struggle to recover, for whose validation he felt driven to identify rules, gave Gregory little or no trouble. He could see straight through them – or rather past them – to the world of the spirit; and return to the letter enlightened by the Spirit. Gregory's allegorical exegesis proceeds from the signified to the signifier; the direction opposite to Augustine's.

To call both Gregory's and Augustine's exegesis – more precisely, some of it – 'allegorical' is to obliterate this fundamental difference in direction. Augustine's explorations sought an opening into a spiritual world half-known, half-disclosed through the scriptural symbols. Gregory's way was the reverse: starting from a spiritual sense much less problematic to him, with a mind full of the knowledge of what the symbols stood for, he returned to the text in the light of the meaning it could be given by this knowledge. His exegetical purpose was to highlight what the text could be made to tell his audience about their lives. Paul Ricoeur has said that

> Medieval hermeneutics pursued the coincidence between the understanding of the faith in the *lectio divina* and the understanding of reality as a whole, divine and human, historical and physical . . . Scripture appears here as an inexhaustible treasure which stimulates thought about everything, which conceals a total interpretation of the world . . .[37]

37 *Essays on biblical interpretation*, ed. L. S. Mudge (London, 1981) 52–53. Jean leclercq, *L'amour des lettres et le désir de Dieu* (Paris, 1957), though in his chapter devoted to Gregory the Great he – oddly – does not deal with his interpretation of the scriptures, writes: 'il emprunte à la Bible les images concrètes qui permettent à chacun de reconnaître en ces expériences sa propre aventure' (39).

This far, we may accept Ricoeur's statement; but when he concludes that 'Hermeneutics is the very deciphering of life in the mirror of the text . . .', this seems to be the exact reverse of Gregory's procedure. The allegory is not so much a pulley (see above, n. 19) that lifts the reader to God, as a device which enables the reader who already knows God to return to the text and detect His *vestigia* in it. Gregory does not so much decipher life in the mirror of the text as the text in the mirror of life, the fullest Christian life; and, although it is true that the scripture is an inexhaustible treasure for Gregory, it is not so much that it stimulates his thought about everything, but rather that it will yield its treasure under the stimulus of Christian life lived at its fullest and truest. The enhanced meaning is generated by the reader's interpretative activity: mercilessly atomised bits of text are reassembled to support a spiritual treatise disguised as commentary.

We can now safely conclude that Gregory's and Augustine's exegetical stances were very different – bearing in mind that the comparison is with Augustine's hermeneutic theory and with the exegetical preferences suggested by it, which he was indeed increasingly inclined to follow. Does this then mean any more than that Gregory reverted to the ancient Christian tradition of Clement, Origen,[38] Ambrose and the rest, a tradition even Augustine had not quite managed to jettison entirely? Does it not look as if it was in fact Augustine who had taken another turning, and that old habits quickly re-established themselves once his extraordinary sophistication and theoretical analyses were forgotten? I must concede the force of this objection; but I nevertheless want to suggest that with Gregory, too – as we found with Augustine – the stance adopted towards the text reveals something more fundamental and more general about how Gregory saw his world. What I have suggested so far in this lecture is that compared with Augustine, Gregory found the text before him far more

38 On Gregory and Origen see Matter, *The voice of my beloved*, 94.

transparent, the meaning behind it – its 'spiritual' or 'figurative' sense – far more readily accessible and the immediate, 'literal' meaning of far less interest. I shall now go on to a second point: that Gregory's, like Augustine's, habits of reading the scriptures reflected the ways in which he looked at the world.

Reading, seeing and participating

Not sharing Augustine's interest in problems about meaning, in how texts are understood and how objects can function as signs, Gregory's views on these things have to be approached indirectly. We can do so through an examination of his views on a subject which has been much discussed in recent years – the way we see pictures.[39] Fortunately, Gregory himself provides a clue when he compares understanding the senses of the scriptures to seeing a picture:[40]

> For the way sacred scripture is both in the words and in their meanings is like the way that a picture is both in its colours and in the things [represented]. Somebody who

39 See C. M. Chazelle, 'Pictures, books and the illiterate: Pope Gregory I's letters to Serenus of Marseilles', *Word and image* 6 (1990) 138–53; H. L. Kessler, 'Pictorial narrative and church mission in sixth century Gaul', *Studies in the history of art* 16 (*Pictorial narrative in Antiquity and the Middle Ages*, ed. H. L. Kessler & M. S. Simpson, 1985) 75–91; P. A. Mariaux, 'L'image selon Grégoire le Grand et la question de l'art missionaire', *Cristianesimo nella storia* 14 (1993) 1–12; L. G. Duggan, 'Was art really the "book of the illiterate"?', *Word and Image* 5 (1989) 227–51; G. Cavallo, 'Testo e immagine nell'Alto Medioevo', *Settimane di studio del Centro Italiano di Studi sull'Alto Medioevo* 41 (1994) 31–64; and especially an unpublished paper by Peter Brown, 'Images as substitutes for writing'.

40 *In Cant.* 4: *Sic est enim scriptura sacra in verbis et sensibus, sicut pictura in coloribus et rebus: et nimis stultus est, qui picturae coloribus inhaeret, ut res, quae pictae sunt, ignoret. Nos enim, si verba quae exterius dicuntur, amplectimur et sensus ignoramus, quasi ignorantes res quae depictae sunt, solos colores tenemus. Littera occidit, scriptum est, spiritus autem vivificat.*

looks at the colours of a picture only to ignore the things depicted is exceedingly stupid; so, if we hear the words outwardly said and ignore their meaning, we are like people who stick to looking at the colours without knowing what is depicted by the picture.

In other words: to stick with the sign without looking beyond to the signified – the patches of colour without what the picture represents, or the biblical text without its further meaning – is exceedingly stupid. Gregory's analogy is straightforward, and, indeed, except for its less precise language, very much in line with the theory of signification elaborated by Augustine in his *De doctrina Christiana*.[41] But the way Gregory applies the sign-signified relation to seeing a picture is very different from Augustine's. Consider the most detailed of Augustine's discussions, one in which he is actually concerned with the way we see a miracle. Augustine introduces the way we see pictures as an analogy to clarify what he is saying about miracles:

> . . . let us seek its profundity; let us not take delight merely in its surface appearance (*superficie*) but also examine its depth. For that which we admire on the outside (*foris*), contains something within (*intus*) . . . Just as if we were to look at some beautiful lettering somewhere, it would not be enough for us to praise the calligrapher's skill in making the letters so uniform, regular and beautiful, if we did not also read what he has indicated by their means; likewise, someone who merely beholds a deed (*factum*) takes pleasure in its beauty so that he praises its author, whereas someone who understands it as it were reads [the sense of the letters]. For a picture is seen in one way, letters in another. When you see a picture, to see it is to appreciate it (*totum vidisse*

41 Cf. Celia Chazelle's discussion, 'Pictures' (see above, n. 39), 146–47.

laudasse); when you see letters, this is not all, for you are bidden also to read them.[42]

This looks like Gregory, but examined more carefully, there is an important difference. Augustine insists that we do *not* see a picture the way we read letters. Understanding a miracle is like reading a script and understanding its meaning, not like seeing a picture and appreciating it in seeing. The difference between Augustine and Gregory is this: Augustine treats seeing a picture as a complete, self-contained, experience, without further reference; we do not see patches of colour which signify the things represented in the painting. But that precisely is how Gregory applied the analogy between a picture and writing. He treats looking at a picture as a double experience: seeing patches of colour, and understanding their meaning. In his account, we *read* a picture the way we read a written text. Now I do not suppose that Gregory would really have thought that what he saw in front of him was a series of patches of colours, which signified a picture representing whatever it was. If asked, he would probably have said – like Augustine – what I see is a picture. What, however, is surely significant is that when he wanted to apply his analogy, he broke down the experience in the way he did. In order to be able to use the analogy with reading a script, Gregory had to divide the experience of looking at a picture; and to divide it in such a way that two elements were involved, a set of signs and their meaning.

What I wish to suggest is that this is characteristic of his pattern of thinking. For Gregory the visible object is there to be seen through, or seen past. Look again at the end of the passage we have been considering about the analogy of seeing a picture and reading:

> if we hear the words outwardly said and ignore their meaning, we are like people who stick to looking at the colours without knowing what is depicted by the picture.

42 *Tr. in Ioh. Ev.* 24.2.

We might expect this to imply that reading a text of the scriptures we think of its meaning. And this is indeed what we find; but the meaning is not the clear, direct, literal meaning, but their remote, 'spiritual' sense; the meaning of the things they stand for – what Augustine would have called their 'figurative' or 'transferred' sense. And to ground this leap in meaning Gregory goes on to quote St Paul's 'The letter killeth but the Spirit giveth life' (2 Cor. 3:6).[43] In Gregory's analogy the *res* referred to by the word, its referent, is elided; he jumps straight to the 'something else' (*aliud aliquid*) signified not by the word, but by the thing signified by the word. Gregory's use of the Pauline antithesis of letter and spirit was exactly like Augustine's in his early writings, an interpretation which, as we have seen, he frankly rejected in his later works.

We can judge how deeply embedded in his mind this habit is from what he says about the meaning of words. In his not infrequent remarks on this subject Gregory often uses Augustine's language; but he systematically misconstrues Augustine's intention. In the Preface to Book IV of the *Moralia*, for instance, he uses language with strong Augustinian overtones:

> When we surmise one thing from another, we easily recognise in the words that what they voice is one thing, what they intimate is another.[44]

This echoes the language of Augustine's distinction between the 'word that sounds outwardly' and the 'word that shines within' (the echo is most striking in the Latin). Augustine had adopted an old Stoic distinction to distinguish a 'word which

43 On Augustine, see Chapter I above, n. 29. Gregory's use of the verse is in line with Augustine's early interpretation: *Mor.* XI.16; XVIII.39; *In Cant.* 4; *In I Lib. Reg.* I.56; IV.123.

44 *Mor.* IV. Praef. 1: *Dum enim alia ex aliis colligimus, facile in eius verbis agnoscimus, aliud esse quod intimant, aliud quod sonant.* Cf. *ibid.*, *Exterius rationabile son[are] . . . studium interioris intellectus accende[re].* (My translation inverts the order of the either/or to bring out the parallel with Augustine's distinction.)

sounds outward' from a 'word luminous within', the former being a sign signifying the latter; a spoken word signifying a mental word, perhaps we should say a concept.[45] This distinction, however, is quite alien to Gregory. He uses Augustine's terminology, but for a totally different purpose: to distinguish the literal sense of a text from its 'inner', 'spiritual' or 'figurative' sense. Thus commenting on the verse 'They brought the child to Eli' (1 Sam. 1:25), Gregory writes:

> What does it mean in saying that the boy Samuel was brought to Eli unless it is what is clearly known, that whoever seeks to profit others by preaching, must know not only the new things but also the old? Wherefore the Lord also says in the gospel parable: 'Therefore every scribe who has been trained for the kingdom of heaven is like a householder who brings out of his treasure what is new and what is old' (Matt. 13:24). Samuel is then offered to Eli when the mind of somebody who is subject to the law is making progress in knowledge of the prophets. In the old books he reads the letter that kills, but understands in it the spirit that gives life (2 Cor. 3:6). Thus he receives the words that sound outside, so that beyond the sound of the syllables he also recognises the spirit which resounds within . . .

and so he will come to the faith which is corroborated in the New Testament.[46] The word is a sign not of the concept it expresses, but of a further, more remote meaning: its 'spiritual' or 'figurative' sense, which is its 'inner' sense.

Gregory systematically transposes Augustine's conception

---

45 On Augustine's distinction between the *verbum quod foris sonat* and the *verbum quod intus lucet* (*De Trin*. XV.11.20) see my paper 'Augustine on signs', *Phronesis* 2 (1957) 76–78, reprinted in *Sacred and secular* (London, 1994) XIV = Chapter 3 below; see especially pp. 94–95.

46 *In I Reg*. I.56: the last sentence of the passage quoted reads: *et sic quod foris sonat accipiat, ut praeter elementorum sonum quod intus insonet spiritus recognoscat*. See also *Mor*. XXV.16.41; XXVI.10.15; *Hom. in Ez*. II.10.1.

of signification in such a way that the meaning of any sign is one stage behind the clear and direct meaning. This should not surprise us, now that we are familiar with Gregory's cast of mind. It coheres with his favourite habit of interpretation: the meaning of a text is primarily its inner, spiritual meaning; its literal sense is readily eclipsed, holding comparatively little interest for him. The text, like any element of experience, comes charged with the shimmering presence of what is behind it or beyond it. Transparent to our reading, the text tends, so to speak, to erase itself in the presence of the meaning it reveals.

Deep-rooted habits of ascetic reading of the biblical text predisposed Gregory, like many Christians in the sixth century and later, to distance themselves from the world of their immediate experience. Peter Brown has likened this to a shift from 'presence' (*praesentia*) to 'representation' (*pictura*), with the corresponding shift in attitude from 'participation' to 'reading'. The presences became messages, the pictures asked for a 'chaste act of reading', from a safe distance. We are dealing here with a huge change in Christian sensibility, which Peter Brown describes as 'a watershed in the Christian imagination that falls somewhere in the late sixth century'.[47] Augustine and Gregory were on opposite sides of this watershed.

Perhaps we should also see the eschatological perspective in which Gregory tends to see his world against this background.[48] Convinced of the crumbling away of the fabric of the material world around him, of the remnants of the Roman past, he was driven to look beyond: even if we had no Gospel to tell us, the world itself proclaims the truth – its ruins are its

47 In 'Images as a substitute for writing' (see above, n. 39).
48 See my paper 'The sacred and the secular: from Augustine to Gregory the Great', *JThS* n.s. 36 (1985) 84–96 (repr. in *The Sacred and the secular*, II); and C. Dagens, 'La fin des temps et l'Église selon S. Grégoire le Grand', *RechSR* 58 (1970) 273–88.

voice, warning us not to love it.[49] The troubled earth itself 'has become as it were the page of a book'.[50] Gregory's way to a world beyond our tangible everyday world is altogether quicker and more direct. God's creatures do not have to be put to the question in order to serve as signs of God's presence: 'Although we cannot yet see Him, we are nevertheless on our way to seeing Him if we admire Him in the things he has made. We call creatures His "footsteps" (*vestigia*) because . . . following them we come to Him.'[51] In a passage very reminiscent of Augustine, Gregory comments on the verse 'Who does not know that the hand of the Lord has done this?' (Job 12:9):

> . . . all proclaim God to be the creator of all . . . This may also be understood literally (*iuxta solam speciem litterae*): for each creature when looked at gives as it were its own testimony, [by means of] the very form it has (*ipsam quam habet speciem suam*). Cattle, birds, the earth or fish, if we ask them while we look, reply with one voice that the Lord made everything. While they imprint their form (*species*) on our senses they proclaim that they are not from themselves. By the very fact that they are created, they proclaim by the form they manifest (*per ostensam speciem*) their creator: [this is] as it were the voice of their confession . . .[52]

This is so reminiscent of Augustine's splendid chapter about the testimony given by creatures to their creator in the

49 *Hom. in Ev.* I.4.2; cf. I.5.1; I.1.1–5.

50 *Ep.* III.29.

51 *Mor.* XXVI.12.17–18; cf. *Hom. in Ez.* II.5.10. To this there are, of course, parallels in Augustine, e.g. *De civ. Dei* XI.28; but more often Augustine stresses the negative (as in *vestigia tua non cognoscerentur –Enarr. in Ps.* 76.21–22), or – almost invariably in his Sermons – to following Christ's *vestigia* (as in *Sermo* 37.16). *Mor.* XVI.33.41 combines the two images.

52 *Mor.* XI.4.6. Compare Augustine, *Conf.* X.6.9. Cf. above, Chapter 1, n. 74.

Confessions that it is hard not to be convinced there was a memory of it in Gregory's mind. What is missing in Gregory's echo of it is the denial Augustine immediately appends: this is not self-evident 'to all who are of sound mind'. Gregory does not for a moment doubt that it will indeed be evident to all: created things for him are transparent without any need to question and to judge the creatures' response.

As we found with Augustine, the way Christians read the scriptures was linked at a profound level with the way they looked at the world around them. This has long been understood by scholars who have approached our theme from the other end, seeking to understand changing attitudes to images 'in the context of a general intellectual realignment'.[53] Averil Cameron's outstanding studies of this theme have located very precisely the issues at the centre of the debate over the status and power of the visible image, the icon: 'the Christian argument itself was about signification, what signified, and how'.[54] The shift in the intellectual horizons since Augustine's time was, among other things, a shift in the way the world and the biblical text were related. For Augustine, to understand the meaning of a text you needed to know its language; if it is poetic, metaphorical or allegorical, you would have needed the skills of the *grammaticus* to unravel them. Likewise, to perceive the world around you you must be able to see, hear and touch. But to understand the events of the Old Dispensation in the light of the New, or to recognise created things as pointing to their Creator, you needed to be converted. Then the things you read about and the things you saw and handled would become divine books for you.[55] For Gregory there was

---

53 Averil Cameron, 'The language of images: the rise of icons and Christian representation', in *The Church and the arts*, ed. Diana Wood (*SCH* 28. Oxford, 1992) 1–42; quotation from p. 33.

54 *Ibid.*, 37.

55 *Enarr. in Ps.* 45.7: *Liber tibi sit pagina divina, ut haec audias; liber tibi sit orbis terrarum ut haec videas.* Cf. J. Pépin, 'Saint Augustin et la fonction protréptique de l'allégorie', *RechAug* 1 (1958) 243–86.

nothing so demanding about the process whereby the scriptural text, its symbols, the world of creatures and its miracles
could become divine books, the texts directly revelatory. The
whole process of signification, of passing from the sign to
signified, was telescoped into a simpler, more direct act of
perception. Texts, like the everyday things around us, would
dissolve in the light of what they have revealed. Like Byzantine icons, the signs 'are not symbols in the usual sense of the
term – when one thing stands for another – but, to quote
Lossky, real 'material signs of the presence of the spiritual
world'.[56] The intellectual realignment that made this shift
possible had taken place by Gregory's time; and it involved, as
Averil Cameron put it, 'the replacement of the existing
vestiges of classical culture by a codification of knowledge
based on religious truth'.[57]

   In these two chapters I have been trying to find some way of
understanding a huge intellectual upheaval. I have, of course,
confined myself to two towering figures, both of them
Western, Latin-speaking Christians, and this clearly must
count as a powerful brake on generalising my conclusion.
Certainly, whatever cultural and spiritual discontinuity can be
diagnosed in the Latin West affected the Christian culture of
the Byzantine world in a less spectacular way, and more
slowly; but there can be no doubt that analogous shifts took
place there, too. Christian discourse here, too, came to define
the boundaries of experience and the means of describing the
world.[58] The problems about representation, language and
meaning which have been the subject of my lectures were
central to this cultural shift.

---

56 Quoted by Averil Cameron, 'The language of images', 29, from
V. Lossky, *Mystical theology*, 189.
   57 *Ibid.*, 33.
   58 The work of Averil Cameron has done as much as that of any other
scholar to elucidate this. I refer here only to her *Christianity and rhetoric of
empire* (Berkeley, 1991), especially 222–29 for a summary.

Chapter Three
AUGUSTINE ON SIGNS[1]

Many of the topics of Augustinian theology and philosophy
in which the notion of 'signs' is central have received a good
deal of attention. This is true, above all, of Augustine's
sacramental theology. His definition of *sacramentum* in terms
of *signum* became classical. His definition of *signum* is rarely
mentioned by later writers, except in the context of sacramental theology; nevertheless, the notion plays an important part
in other contexts. Chief among these is Augustine's discussion of the meanings of Scripture,[2] but the concept enters
into such diverse fields of his interests as his theory of
language, his discussion of miracles, of the relation of the
world to God, and of man's way of acquiring knowledge, not
least knowledge of himself. Notwithstanding the focal interest of the notions of sign and of meaning in Augustine's
thought, they have, so far as I know, not received treatment
as such. This essay is, therefore, an attempt to disentangle
what Augustine thought about signs, in particular, about
words, and meaning. At the risk of ascribing to him preoccu-
pations which he would scarcely have recognised, no attempt
is made here to deal with any of the applications made by
Augustine of the notion.

1 I have to thank Professor A. H. Armstrong (Liverpool) and Professor
Christine Mohrmann (Nijmegen) for valuable suggestions in writing this
paper.
2 H.-M. Féret has, I think, established that it was from this field that
Augustine came to see the possibilities of a sacramental theology formulated in terms of *signum*. See his '*Res* dans la langue théologique de saint
Augustin', in *Rev. des sciences phil. et théol.* 29 (1940) 218–43.

Background in Hellenistic thought

A survey of the relevant background of discussion, here as in general,[3] serves to throw into relief the originality of Augustine's contribution. From Aristotle onwards, the theme of 'signs' recurs regularly in Greek philosophy; indeed, Philodemus in his *De signis* and Sextus Empiricus suggest that the question of signs was one of the focal points of the Stoic–Epicurean debate.[4] The broad terms of reference for the debate had been set by Aristotle's discussion of arguments *ex eikotôn* (from images) and *ek' sêmeiôn* (from signs). This is the context in which he defines *sêmeion* as *protasis apodeiktikê ê anankaia ê endoxos* (a sign is a demonstrative premiss, either necessary or probable; *Anal. Prior.* II.27.70a7). Anything which involves in its being the being of something else, either at the same time or before or later, is a 'sign' of that thing or event. The classification of the types of argument from signs which Aristotle goes on to give, and their analysis, do not concern us here. It should be noted, however, that this is the concept of sign which recurs in rhetorical contexts, first in Aristotle (cf. *de Soph. Elench.* 167b9; *Rhet.* I. 1357 a32–b36), and after him in almost every ancient work on rhetoric.[5]

Notwithstanding important variations, the Aristotelian theory of signs as a means of inference sets the general framework for the Stoic and Epicurean treatment. In both schools, signs are the means of inference from what is empirically given (*prodêlon*) to what is non-apparent (*adêlon*). The slightly different classifications of *adêla* given by the two

---

3 See H.-I. Marrou, *Saint Augustin et la fin de la culture antique* (Paris, 1938).

4 For a general account, cf. P. H. and E. A. de Lacy, *Philodemus: on methods of inference* (Philadelphia, 1941), especially 157–78; E. A. de Lacy, 'Meaning and methodology in Hellenistic philosophy', *Phil. Rev.* 47 (1938) 390–409; and P. H. de Lacy, 'The Epicurean analysis of language', *Amer. J. of Philology* 60 (1939) 85–92.

5 Cf. P. H. and E. A. de Lacy, *Philodemus . . .*, 133.

schools, and the different kinds of inference admitted by them as legitimate, need not detain us here,[6] as we are not concerned with the differences of opinion about the reach of knowledge or the means of obtaining it. Stoic logic (*dialektikê*) was defined, in one way, as the science 'about signs and things signified' (*peri sêmainonta kai sêmainomena* – Diog. Laert. vii.62). Its definition of 'sign' as 'a proposition in sound condition which is antecedent and revelatory of the conclusion' (Sext. Emp. *Adv. math.* viii.245) is cast in prepositional terms[7] in accordance with the Stoic view of reason and the metaphysical structure of the world. The latter is a deterministic system in which things are connected by rational necessity. Events are logically connected with other events, and the sign therefore analytically entails the thing or event signified.[8] Hence the Stoic insistence on the intervention of a conceptual intermediary between the sign and the thing signified in the sign-relation: a sign signifies its object in virtue of a concept which applies to the object signified (Sext. Emp. *Adv. math.* viii.11–12).

The Epicurean theory does away with this conceptual intermediary (*ibid.*, 13),[9] and in this denial is centred its opposition to the intellectualised character of the sign in Stoic logic. Sextus Empiricus states the divergence between the two schools as lying in the fact that one conceives signs as intellectual, the other as sensible entities (*ibid.*, 177). Accordingly, for Epicurean logic, the relation of sign to thing signified is not a logical nexus; the inference from one to the

6 Cf. Sext. Emp. *Adv. math.* viii.145–47 and 316–24; Philod. *De signis*, frag. 4.

7 A sign has the form 'If p then q'; cf. Sext. Emp. *Adv. math.* viii.276.

8 Cf. Sext. Emp. *Pyrrh. Hyp.* B. 111–13.

9 Philodemus criticises an ambiguity in the Stoics' usage of 'sign', which, he says, they use to mean the appearance from which an inference is made as well as to mean the inference itself (*De signis* col. 36). It is easy to see how the Stoic location of the sign-signified relation on the conceptual level could lead to this ambiguity.

other is based on *prolêpsis* (anticipation; Diog. Laert. X.33–34), and this kind of mental association is likewise the source of words having fixed meanings. Simple empirical sequence is at the root of the sign-signified relation: a regular and observed sequence establishes the *prolêpsis* which enables an inference to be made from one to the other, and such inference is valid only where there is a possibility of verification in sense (*epimartyrêsis* – cf. Sext. Emp. *Adv. math.* vii.212–16). By this means inference can extend the bounds of knowledge beyond the limits of what is given in present sense-experience to what may be verified in the future.

The Epicurean theory of signs, which derived their meaning from *prolêpsis*, had no difficulty in accounting for the phenomena of language as well as of naturally expressive activity such as instinctive cries of beasts and men, gesture, and their like.[10] It is not clear to what extent the Stoic theory of signs was meant by its adherents to provide a theory of language; at any rate, Diogenes Laertius is able to call the Stoic logic (*dialektikê*), defined by Chrysippus, as he notes, as the study of signs and things signified, their 'theory of language' (*hê peri phônês theôria* – vii.62). Its inadequacy in this field – in so far as it is pressed into service to furnish a theory of language – is apparent. Thus one line of attack made on the Stoic theory of signs by Sextus Empiricus is the observation that it cannot account for instinctive and non-discursive response to and interpretation of signs, being exclusively propositional and inferential in character (*Adv. math.* viii.269–71), and that it is therefore unsuitable for any theory of language which would take into account behaviour of this type. For his own part, Sextus Empiricus is quite ready to include words among 'admonitive signs' (*sêmeia hypomnêstika* – *Adv. math.* viii.289–90). These, admitted by him as a legitimate basis for inferring 'temporarily non-apparent

10 Cf. Diog. Laert. X.75–76; Lucret. *De rer. nat.* V.1028ff.

things' (*pros kairon adêla*), bring to mind the thing signified on experiencing its sign, in virtue of their regularly observed association. The 'indicative sign' (*sêmeion endeiktikon*),[11] however, is never observed in conjunction with the object signified – which is *physei adêlon* (non-apparent by nature) and hence never observed along with its sign – and cannot therefore serve as the basis of an inference.[12] It is only this latter kind of sign that he attacks, and as he is careful to note, his attack leaves the kind of sign of which language consists untouched.

This brief outline must serve as a summary of a sustained debate, of which Augustine can have had little first-hand knowledge. Nevertheless, it is against its background that his theory of signs must be assessed. Although the logical acumen brought to bear on the problems of inference from signs by Stoic and Epicurean writers was to be eclipsed by other interests, the general outlines of their discussion served to define the scope of 'signs' in the scraps of theory about them to be found in later writers, secular and ecclesiastic alike. The definition, for instance, given by Cicero in the context of an examination of 'probable arguments' is a direct echo of the Aristotelian definition[13] combined with the Epicurean insistence on the need for verification: *signum est quod sub sensum aliquem cadit et quiddam significat quod ex ipso profecto videtur, quod aut ante fuerit aut in ipso negotio aut post sit consecutum, et tamen indiget testimonii et gravioris confirmationis* . . . (a sign is something which falls under one of the senses and signifies something that is directly evident from it, which either preceded it, or follows it either immediately or later, but nevertheless requires testimony or more secure

---

11 Which *antikrys ek tês idias physeôs kai kataskeuês monon oukhi phônên aphien legetai* [by the Stoics] *sêmainein to 'ou estin endeiktikon*, *ibid.*, 154.

12 For this discussion, see *Adv. math.*, viii.145–58.

13 Cf. above, p. 72.

confirmation; *de Inv.* i.30).[14] Quintilian, likewise, in his classification of *probationes artificiales* (artificial proofs) defines signs as one of the possible bases of inference *(Inst. Or.* v.9). In general it may safely be asserted that this is the sense which *signum* and *sêmeion* actually bear in the contexts where they are used. According to the particular field of application, they can normally be translated by 'evidence', 'symptom', 'portent'[15] – a 'sign' always allows something else to be inferred. The same general acceptance is found again in ecclesiastical writers;[16] a notable and frequently recurring instance is the usage of 'signs' in reference to Scriptural events seen by the writers as pointing to other events. A strand of complexity is, however, often discernible in the application of the word 'sign' to the biblical miracles. Origen, in his comment on why *sêmeion* rather than *teras* (wonder) is the appropriate word for these, suggests the reason why this class of instances forms no exception to the rule: *ouk esti paradoxon genomenon en tê Graphê, ho mê esti sêmeion kai symbolon heterou para to aisthêtôs gegenêmenon* (nothing paradoxical happens in the scripture that is not a sign or a symbol of something else; *In Joann.* 13.60, *PG* 14.521): miracles are 'signs' and not mere 'wonders' precisely because by their marvellous nature they direct the mind to their author and his meaning in bringing them about. Another passage from Origen is worth quoting, if only because it is sometimes suggested that this may have been the source of Augustine's definition of signs: *signum namque dicitur, cum per hoc quod videtur aliud aliquid indicatur* . . . (a sign is said to be

14 On Cicero's attitude to the Epicurean Philodemus, cf. J. F. d'Alton, *Roman literary theory* (London, 1931) 160.

15 Cf. Cicero, *de Div., passim* (the reference in I.3.6 to Zeno's lost work *peri Sêmeiôn* may be either to a work on divination or to a logical treatise); Stob. *Ecl.* II.122, 238; Macrob. *Comm. in Somn.* I.xxix.27 and *Saturn.* xvii.3; Plotinus, *Enn.* II.3.3.10; II.9.13; III.1.5; III.3.1 etc.

16 Cf. *I Clem.* 12.7; *Did.* 16.6; Clem. Al. *Strom.* 8.6 (*PG* 9.585C); Basil, *Ep.* 260.8 (*PG* 32.965B) etc.

something which by being seen indicates something else; *In Rom.* 4.2, *PG* 14.968).

Some of the contexts, then, in which ecclesiastical writers used the notion of signs, though radically new, were still built around the notion understood in the general sense as current from Aristotle onwards. In the typological exegesis of the Bible by St Hilary and St Ambrose – above all a formative influence on Augustine – *signum* acquired a whole range of new resonances.[17] Nonetheless, the usage still remained within the scope of the definitions we have noticed in Cicero, Quintilian and Origen.

It will have appeared from this summary survey of Hellenistic reflection about signs and its traces in Roman rhetoric and Christian theology, that the theory of signs is conceived primarily as a theory of inference. Language is hardly mentioned in this context,[18] and when it is explicitly recognised as relevant – since words *signify* and are therefore inescapably signs – the linguistic interest is only incidental. We have noted, for instance, that when Sextus Empiricus defines words as belonging to the class of *sêmeia hypomnêstika*, he does so in order to forestall the objection that his rejection of *sêmeia endeiktika* would involve the rejection of verbal signs, an obvious absurdity (*Adv. math.* viii.289–90; cf. above, pp. 74–75). Aristotle, in defining words in terms of *symbolon* (*de Int.* I.16a), may have been concerned to avoid the term *sêmeion*, already in the process of becoming a technical word in his discussion of inference; though a few lines further on he does use *sêmeion* in reference to verbs (16b7–10). In general, no one would dispute that words are signs; but for no writer is the theory of signs primarily a theory of language, nor is reflection on language carried on in terms of 'signs'.

17 For a discussion of the terminology of typology, cf. J.-P. Brisson's introduction to his edition of the *Tractatus Mysteriorum* attributed to Hilary of Poitiers, in *Sources Chrétiennes* (Paris, 1947).

18 We shall have to return to a discussion of language in pre-Augustinian writers in another context; cf. below, pp. 91–93.

Before Augustine, I have found only one hint of an attempt to bring the notion of 'signification' to a central place in a theory of language. It occurs in a brief suggestion made by Plotinus which might well have been known to Augustine.[19] In his discussion of the categories of being, Plotinus asks to what category do words belong. His account is a criticism of Aristotle's statement (*Categ.* VI.4b32–35) that since speech is measured by syllables, it is a *poson* (quantity). Plotinus admits that it is *metrêton* (measured), but denies that, as *logos*, it is a *poson*. The reason he gives is that, as such, it is significant (*sêmantikon*). He then goes on to suggest that from the material point of view, speech consists of the disturbance set up by the voice in the surrounding air, and therefore falls into the category of action, so that it should be defined as 'meaningful action' (*poiêsis sêmantikê* – *Enn.* VI.1.5).

It is scarcely possible – and, in view of Augustine's preoccupation with language of which he tells us in the first Book of his *Confessions*, scarcely necessary – to trace back to this hint the central place he gives to language in his reflection on signs. A more powerful influence which would tend to suggest a theory of language conceived in terms of a theory of signs was, in all probability, the primacy in Augustine's interests of Scriptural 'signs'. A theory of language as a system of signs must have been tempting, since it secured the possibility of bringing under one head, that of 'signs', the two enquiries into the literal meaning and the figurative or typological sense of Scripture. At any rate, whatever the reasons, words are for Augustine, signs *par excellence*, and his theory of signs is meant to be, from the start, a theory of language as well as of other types of sign. In this consists the originality of his reflection on meaning, and its ability to focus so many of his interests.

19 Cf. P. Henry, *Plotin et l'Occident* (Paris, 1934) 55, 228–29; although there appear to be no direct allusions to this treatise in Augustine, it was well known to Victorinus.

The interpreting of signs: the Interior Teacher

Augustine's first *ex professo* discussion of the meaning of signs occurs in the early *De magistro*. This work, dated about 389, is a dialogue, genuine and historical as Augustine claims in the *Confessions*,[20] between himself and his son Adeodatus.[21]

The enquiry concerns the meaning of signs, and of spoken words in particular, which are the most common and most important sort of sign. Why do we use signs? – is Augustine's opening question. The purpose of all speaking, we are told, is 'either to teach or to remind others or ourselves' (*De mag.* I.1). Other apparent purposes, such as for instance asking questions in order to learn, can all be brought under these two heads: for in asking questions we do no more than teach other people what we want to know. But there are more serious objections to be answered, the answers to which give some hint of how wide a range of functions will be ascribed to 'reminding' and to *memoria* (which I am content, for the present purpose, to render by the word 'memory'). Thus the objection has to be met that Christ taught his disciples to pray in set forms of words, whereas God can have no need of being taught or reminded of men's needs and desires. This difficulty is solved by agreeing that Christ 'did not teach them words, but realities by means of words. Thus they were to remind themselves to whom to pray and what to pray for . . .' (*De mag.* I.2). With such a broad acceptance of *memoria* nothing is in the way of establishing as a conclusion to Chapter I that 'even when we merely strain our minds towards something,

20 *Conf.* IX.6.14.
21 The date of the conversation appears to be about a year after their conversion, so Adeodatus must have been about sixteen at the time. *Horrori mihi erat illud ingenium* (I was astonished at his intelligence) Augustine exclaims in the *Confessions*, writing of Adeodatus's precocious intellectual power; and indeed, it is difficult, in reading the record of this conversation, not to take Adeodatus's side time and again in his refusal to acquiesce in some of his father's more palpable sophistries.

although we utter no sound, yet because we ponder the words themselves, we do speak within our own minds. So, too, speech is a recalling to mind, since the memory in which the words are stored, by considering them, brings to mind the realities themselves of which the words are signs' (*ibid.*). Thus speech puts before the mind what was previously either altogether absent from it, or at least not present to it in the sense of being actually thought about.

This then is the common ground from which proceeds the enquiry begun in Chapter II of what words 'signify' (II.3). The first part of the argument, extending over the following five chapters and summarised in Chapter VIII, is designed to establish, first, that signs are the indispensable means of directing the mind's attention to things, and that nothing, therefore, can be learnt without the use of signs (III.6; cf. X.29–31). The meaning of a sign, what it 'signifies', can only be expounded and established by means of further signs, as it were by giving synonyms; by circumlocution; by pointing or gesture; or by pictorial representation. The only exceptions granted at this stage in the discussion are words standing for actions, the meaning of which can be illustrated by actually performing the actions named by the words, for instance by walking or by speaking when one is asked for the meaning of *ambulare* or *loqui*. But even this is taken back later on, when these results established in the first part of the dialogue are recapitulated in the course of the argument of the second part. Adeodatus there rightly points out that such direct illustrative performance cannot be understood as giving the meaning of a word without any sign whatsoever: for it involves that the particular bit of walking done be performed and understood precisely as signifying any instance of walking, at any speed, by anybody, for any distance, etc. (X.29). Even at this point, however, Adeodatus is inclined to except the case of teaching and of speaking, both of which, he thinks, can be directly exemplified; but Augustine induces him to take the final step: 'we have as yet found nothing which can be shown directly by itself except speech, which also signifies itself along with other things. But since speech itself consists of signs, there is still nothing that can be taught without signs' (X.30). To establish this conclusion is the main burden of the first part of the work, and the rest of this part is taken up with a bewildering and often sophistical discussion of the ways in which 'speech also signifies itself along with other things'. To mark the end of this first part of the discussion, Augustine apologises for all this seemingly childish playing with words, but defends it as a prelude intended 'to exercise the power and keenness of our minds (*vires et mentis aciem*) and so to prepare ourselves not only to be able to support, but also to love the warmth and light of the blessed life' *(ibid.*, VIII.21). And so we pass to the second part of the dialogue, which deals with signs signifying not other signs, but things which are not themselves signs but *significabilia* as they had agreed to call them.[22]

This part begins with the long overdue distinction between use and mention, that is to say between, for example, 'man' as being a noun and man as being an animal (VIII.24). To solve the puzzles which arise from neglecting this distinction Adeodatus points out that 'the things we speak of, we signify; and what comes forth from the mouth of the speaker is not the reality signified but the sign by which it is signified' (VIII.23). Neither of the speakers seem to be aware of the relevance of this observation to the first part of the discussion. Adeodatus goes on to deny the applicability to words of the distinction just drawn between use and mention: 'the exception [to this rule] is when it is the signs themselves that are signified, a class we treated of a little while ago' (VIII.23). These exceptions apart, then, in general we use words to talk about the things they stand for, in order to gain and to communicate knowledge about them (IX); and indeed, as the first part of the argument claims to have established already, nothing can be

22 . . . *ea quae signis significari possunt et signa non sunt . . ., ibid.*, IV.8.

learnt without signs, not even things which can be directly illustrated by the teacher (X.29–31).

What happens, then, in the course of a conversation when a word or phrase crops up whose meaning is not understood by one of the parties?

> Thus when I read the words *et saraballae eorum non sunt immutatae*, the word *saraballae* does not manifest to me the reality which it signifies. If it is headcoverings of some sort that are called by this name, did I upon hearing this learn either what a head or what coverings are? These I had known before; and my knowledge of them was gained not when they were called such by others but when they were seen by myself. The first time the two syllables *caput* struck my ears, I was just as ignorant of what they signified as when I first read *saraballae*. But when the word *caput* was repeatedly pronounced, I discovered that it was the word for a thing which was already most familiar to me from sight. Before I made that discovery, this word was a mere noise to me; but I learned that it was a sign, when I discovered what it was a sign of. And that reality I got to know, as I said, not from being signified to me, but by seeing it (*non significatu sed aspectu didiceram*). Therefore, it is the sign that is learnt from the thing rather than the thing from the sign given. (X.33)

Failure in communication, the argument runs, can only be remedied by an explanation of the word or sign which fails in its task of manifesting the reality it signifies; but as the example of *saraballae* shows, such explanation must ultimately reach a point at which direct acquaintance with the *significata* of primitive words is presupposed. In the following paragraph Augustine goes on to generalise this conclusion:

> What I am above all trying to convince you of, if I can, is that we do not learn anything by means of the signs we

call words. For, on the contrary, as I have said, we learn
the meaning of the word (*vim verbi*) – that is to say the
significance that is hidden in the sound – only after
recognising the reality which it signifies; we do not first
perceive this reality by means of such signification.
(X.34)

The pointing with the finger (*intentio digitis*) whereby we
establish the meaning of primitive signs, he maintains, is not a
sign of the reality pointed to, nor of the word which is being
explained by this means, but rather of the indication (*demon-
strationis*) itself. In this way it resembles the function of the
adverb *ecce*. 'By means of the pointing, then, I cannot get to
know either the thing [the head], since I already know that,
nor the sign [the word *caput*], for the finger is not pointed at
that' (X.34).

The conclusion that we cannot get to know the meaning of
signs without knowing the realities they stand for appears to
contradict the conclusion of the first part of the work, namely
that we require signs in order that we may get to know things.
But Augustine means both these positions to be taken quite
seriously, and indeed reiterates the conclusions of the first part
in the course of this argument. His thesis is precisely that no
knowledge can either be acquired or communicated on the
basis of the account so far given: in order that I may know the
meaning of signs, I have to know, in the last resort, the things
they stand for. On the other hand, I have to rely on the words
and signs of teachers to receive the direct experience of these
things – *ut attenderem . . . id est, ut aspectu quaererem quid
viderem* (X.35). 'The value of words, to state the most that can
be said for them, consists in that they bid us look for things.
These they do not display to us for our knowledge' (XI.36).
Either, Augustine seems to be arguing, we get to know the
meaning of words together with the things which exemplify
that meaning, or we have a mere mass of unorganised
experience on the one hand, and a mere series of meaningless

noises on the other. The enquiry after the meaning of symbols is at the same time the enquiry into the reality they speak of: 'If we know [the meaning of words together with the things signified] we recall rather than learn; but if we do not know, we do not even recall, though perhaps we may be prompted to enquire' (XI.36). Human teachers, on the one hand, can only teach us the meanings of words and signs, and experience, on the other hand, only furnishes us with brute givenness. Only the Interior Teacher, which is Christ dwelling in the mind, can teach by at once displaying to the mind the reality to be known and providing the language for its understanding. He is the source of both the objects encountered and the light which illuminates them for our understanding. This is the teacher whose activity is presupposed by all learning. The remaining three chapters are devoted to showing that this Interior Teacher is the source of all truth and knowledge; that he is the invisible light 'which we confessedly consult in regard to visible things, that it may manifest them to us to the extent that we are able to perceive them' (XI.38).

This discussion of signs has, in Augustine's hands, by a metaphysical *tour-de-force*, become one of the buttresses of the doctrine above all associated with his name. The very purpose of the work, as he tells us at the end of his life, had been to show that 'there is no teacher to teach man knowledge but God, according to the teaching of the Gospel: "one is your master, Christ" ' (*Retract.* I.12). This is the avowed concern of the *De magistro* – so much so, that in reviewing it in his *Retractations*, Augustine does not feel called upon even to allude to the theory of signs and meaning which, after all, does form the bulk of it. In trying to isolate and examine this theory it is, therefore, as well to be on one's guard against attributing to it an importance in itself which it would certainly not have had in Augustine's estimation. But it is his theory of signs we are considering, and if we are to do this at all, we must do so on its own merits.

Augustine concluded from the argument of the dialogue

that nothing external to the mind can, in the last resort, be regarded as the source of its knowledge. Neither the crude data of experience nor the 'pointers' to it in language and gesture can give knowledge without what M. Gilson has called[23] the mind's 'irreducible spontaneity'. In the *De magistro* Augustine is content to short-circuit an examination of what this spontaneity consists in by invoking his favourite theory in one of its forms at the crucial point. A further exploration here might have brought him face to face with the inadequacy of a theory of language conceived, as it is in this work, as running parallel to the stream of experience and alongside it, so to speak, rather than within it. There is, indeed, a hint of another view of linguistic expression even in this work, the pursuit of which might have led Augustine to question the adequacy of the picture which is implicit in the rest of the dialogue. This is the suggestion he throws out that certain signs, linguistic or gestural, might be signs of indication, not of objects signified. On this suggestion, a system of signs might contain in itself the 'pointing to' (*intentio*) its objects for which Augustine could find no place in language. But this hint is not developed because, as Augustine says *à propos* of this suggestion, he is not interested in it precisely for the reason, as he puts it, that this pointing is 'only a sign of the indication itself rather than of any things indicated' (*de. Mag.* X.34; above, pp. 82–83). The further development of such a suggestion could have broken through the barrier between signs and *significata*, the mutual externality to each other of language and experience, related only by conventional rules of 'signification'. But by invoking the interpretative activity of the Interior Teacher, Augustine was able to escape the difficulties of this view of language and felt absolved from subjecting it to further scrutiny, at any rate, for the present.

23 *Introduction à l'étude de Saint Augustin* (Paris, 1929) 93.

Symptom and symbol

At the end of the *De magistro* Augustine makes the promise that 'another time, if God wills, we shall examine the whole question of the utility of words, which, properly considered, is not small' (XIV.46). There can be little doubt that the work in which he gives us the fulfilment of this promise is the *De doctrina Christiana*, Books II-IV. In this work, largely written some eight years after the *De magistro*, but not completed until thirty years later,[24] Augustine's discussion is conceived as introductory to and part of his treatise on Scripture interpretation. The work begins with a reminder of what is already familiar from the *De magistro*:

> All knowledge (*doctrina*) is of things or of signs; but things are learnt by means of signs. Here I call *res* primarily only such things as are not used to signify other things, like wood, stone, beast and so on; not, however, the stone on which Jacob rested his head, or the beast sacrificed by Abraham instead of his son. For these, though things, are also signs of further things.
>
> (I.2.2)

Res, in other words, is what a sign signifies directly, even if this *res* should itself happen to be a sign, though in this latter case Augustine prefers not to speak of it as *res* to avoid confusion. Signs, too, he goes on to observe, are *res*, or they would be nothing; but not all *res* are signs. Thus there are things which may be treated under the heads both of *res* and of *signa* according to whether we are interested in them in their own right or in their 'signification'. Certain things, however, have little or no interest in themselves, but their whole importance lies in their being used as signs: such are above all words. This is a considerable advance on the terminology of

24 Written in 397 as far as III.25.35, though the present text may be a revision carried out by Augustine in 427, when the rest of Book III and Book IV were added.

the various types of sign and of *significabilia* agreed in the *De magistro*.[25]

Book I is *de rebus fidem continentibus* (about things that are objects of faith), the rest, as we are told, *De signis* (I.40.44). Augustine's remarks concerning the latter are again prefaced by the warning that we are not to forget that signs, too, are things; but we are now to attend to them in their bearings on other things (II.1.1). A sign, then, in a definition destined to become classical throughout the Middle Ages, is said to be 'a thing which, in addition to what it is perceived to be by the senses (*praeter speciem quam ingerit sensibus*), also brings something else to mind (*in cogitationem*)' (II.1.1). A sign, to paraphrase this definition in more modern language, is an element in a situation in which three terms are related. These we may call the object or *significatum* for which the sign stands, the sign itself, and the subject to whom the sign stands for the object signified.[26] It may be noted in passing that Augustine appears to be the first to have stressed this triadic nature of the relation of "signifying": it had been noticed before that signs belong to the category of relation (*pros ti* – Sext. Emp. *Adv. math.* viii.164); but in all previous discussions the relation of sign to *significatum* is conceived of as a straightforward dyadic relation. The Stoic theory, admittedly, insisted on the presence of a third element in the sign-relation, the *sêmainomenon* or concept signified; the *tungkhanon* or 'object' is signified only indirectly, in so far as this concept applies to it.[27] But no stress was laid on the subject or interpreter to whom the sign means or stands for its object.

A thing is a sign, for Augustine, precisely in so far as it stands *for* something *to* somebody. This three-term relation is

25 Cf. above, n. 22.

26 This paraphrase displays the substantial identity of Augustine's with modern definitions. Cf. Appendix: Note on terminology, pp. 101–04.

27 Cf. above, p. 73. [Added note: see on this my Introduction to the present volume.]

essential to any situation in order that one element in it should function as a sign. A sign-situation is simply a situation in which, among others, this relation obtains. Whatever element in such a situation functions as a sign, may also be related to other elements in the situation in a large variety of other ways. A sign-situation presupposes some of these simpler, two-term relations in which the sign-thing or sign-event must stand to other things or events in order that it may function as a sign. For instance, that smoke may be a sign of fire, its causal dependence on fire independent of any observer is presupposed. Likewise, in order that a noise made by a living organism may be a sign, it must be a product of its activity; and it has to stand in a specific relation to it if it is to be a word with meaning. The triadic relation of 'signifying' is built upon such dyadic relations, and different types of 'signifying' may be distinguished according to what these presupposed two-term relations are in each case.

Augustine distinguishes two fundamental types of sign according to whether the relation of dependence is between the sign and the object, or between the sign and the subject. The first type he calls *signa naturalia*, and defines these as things (or events) 'which from themselves make known something other than themselves without any desire on anybody's part of "signifying"; as, for instance, smoke signifies fire. For smoke is not made by someone wanting to "signify" something, but on being apprehended and noted as a thing experienced, makes known the presence of fire' (II.1.2). As further examples of this class he refers to footprints left by an animal passed out of sight, of facial expressions registering emotions like pain or anger without the person's wishing to show his feelings, and their like. For convenience, and without begging any of the questions that this terminology may suggest, I shall call this type of sign 'symptoms'.[28] A 'symptom', on this usage, which implies a certain extension of

28 Cf. Appendix, below, p. 103.

its sense in normal usage, is anything which 'goes together with' that of which it is taken to be the sign. It may be a 'symptom' in the conventional sense, a 'portent', or 'evidence' in a more general sense; it might depend on its *significatum* as an effect on its cause, as for instance, smoke depends on fire; it might be part of a total condition as a rash is of measles; or it might give rise to its *significatum*, as a southwesterly wind may both bring and signify rain. The sign may be contemporaneous with its *significatum*, or occur before or after it, and the sign-relation may be reversible according to circumstances and observers, and it may be more or less tenuous. But Augustine, as he says, is not concerned with this type of sign, except to distinguish it from the second type, which he calls *signa data*.

These he defines as 'signs which living organisms make to each other in order to indicate, as far as they are able, what they feel or perceive or understand. The only reason we have for "signifying", that is, for giving signs, is to bring forth (*ad depromendum*) what is going on in the mind of the sign-maker and to communicate it (*ad traiciendum*) to another's mind' (II.2.3). Here the thing or event which is the sign is the product of the sign-maker's activity and owes its significance entirely to this. What it means, or more precisely, what he means by it, it means in virtue of what he is doing with it. Let us call signs of this kind 'symbols'.[29] The most important class of 'symbols' is, of course, that of words; not because they differ fundamentally from gesture, facial expression and other forms of expressive activity – all these are *quasi quaedam visibilia verba* (as it were visible words) (II.3.4) – but because words are used solely for the purpose of 'signifying' (I.2.2). They are, so to speak, diaphanous and do not distract attention from what they are employed to mean by claiming attention to what they are in their own right. The sign-signified relation is not here reversible, as it is in the case of

29 Cf. Appendix.

'symptoms', nor is there a causal relation between them on which an inference could be based of the occurrence of the one from the other. On the other hand, a 'symbol' has the determinate meaning or range of meanings which the sign-maker's activity bestows on it. These ways in which 'symbols' differ from 'symptoms' are fundamental, and must not be allowed to be blurred by the fact that there are signs which look as if they might belong to either one or the other class. Instances of such signs are, as Augustine notes in this connection, sounds whereby animals communicate to one another their desires, their perceptions of food or danger and so forth, and also signs like the facial expressions of a man in pain. Whether these are to be treated in the class of 'symbols' or of 'symptoms', that is to say, whether they are to be treated as the products of intentional expressive activity or as involuntary reactions to stimulus and states of feeling, this, he observes, 'is another question and is not relevant to what we are now dealing with' (II.2.3).

'What we are now dealing with' is the distinction between the two fundamentally different types of sign. The question of fact, as to which of the two types certain doubtful cases belong, is, admittedly, a different question. But it is surely not as irrelevant to an enquiry into language as Augustine seems inclined to think that something which looks so very much like language might in fact be something *toto coelo* different. For clearly, although human speech cannot be thought of as a succession of signs in the sense we have called 'symptoms' – for understanding a speaker is not diagnosing from vocal symptoms 'what is biting him'; yet, a good deal of human behaviour is to be understood in more or less this way; and speech as it is actually spoken, or better, acted, in a context of posture, facial expression, gesture, vocal colour, stress and rhythm, involves a good deal of what looks from the outside just like 'symptoms' of feeling. Indeed, it may well be argued that the key to understanding the emergence of the more sophisticated, conventional expressive activity of articulate language is to be found in the primitive 'naturally' meaningful activity of instinctive response: the foundations of deliberate meaningful activity are laid in the growth of awareness of the nexus of feeling (or stimulus) and response and of the possibility of the response being reproduced voluntarily.[30] The two types of sign distinguished in Augustine's dichotomy describe, on the one hand, what happens when we interpret a reaction to a stimulus, and on the other what we do when we interpret, say, a message in Morse Code or a page of the *Principia Mathematica*: but is what we do when listening to human speech very much like either of these activities, or even like a mixture of the two?

Unfortunately, beyond distinguishing the two types of sign and noting their precarious margins, Augustine does not discuss the importance of these cases which may, *prima facie*, be treated as either symptomatic or symbolic in their meaning. He seems to have been content to fall back on the traditional bifurcation of meaning: 'by nature' and 'by convention', although he applies this in a novel way within the framework of his theory of the two kinds of sign. The classical discussion of the question in Plato's *Cratylus* stands in the background;[31]

30 This position is argued at length by Canon E. Masure in *Le signe – passage du visible à l'invisible* (Paris, 1954), a work which is truly Augustinian at least in the scope it ascribes to the notion of 'sign'. On the emergence of deliberate from instinctively meaningful activity, cf. particularly Chapters 5–9. It is instructive to re-read Augustine's account of the process of learning to speak in Book I of the *Confessions* in the light of Masure's suggestions.

31 This statement needs qualification: the *Cratylus* is concerned with the relation of language to thought, and in asking whether words are related to their objects *physei* or *kata synthêkên*, Plato raises a metaphysical question. Epicurus, however, traces two chronologically distinct stages in the emergence of language (Diog. Laert. X.75–76): in the more primitive stage, utterance is the natural response to *pathê* and *phantasmata* impinging on awareness; from this, the need for inter-tribal communication led to the emergence of conventional language. Lucretius stresses the first stage of this process almost exclusively, though his interest is also in the continuity of significance *physei* and *thesei* (cf. *De rer. nat.* v.102ff). Bailey traces the

the Stoic and Epicurean divergences on this topic were, again, a commonplace of which Augustine probably had information at second hand.[32] Having brought the two discussions, that of signs as bases of inference and that of language, under one heading, that of signs, and distinguished the two main types of them, Augustine seems not to have concerned himself further with the question whether words had their meaning *physei* (by nature) or *thesei* (by convention). He merely assumed that in so far as signs have their meaning *physei*, they are *signa naturalia*, and not, properly speaking, language. His unified treatment of signs of all kinds seems to have been purchased at the cost of oversimplifying the problem of linguistic meaning: the distinction between alternative foundations for meaning within language became identified, in his mind, with the distinction between linguistic and extra-linguistic meaning.

Having dismissed *signa naturalia*, Augustine is thus led to describe the meaning of *signa data* as exclusively conventional in nature. He argues, for instance, when discussing the mysterious efficacy of magical invocations, that any expression, to be meaningful, presupposes a social solidarity between users of the same language. The language they both use has meaning *non natura, sed placito et consensione significandi* (not by nature but by decision and agreement on meaning), and is understood just in so far as this *societatis consensio* (agreement of society) is accepted and shared by

---

history of Epicurean thought on this topic and indicates the existence of divergence on both sides of the central Epicurean position. Cf. *The Greek atomists and Epicurus* (Oxford, 1928) 382. On the different perspectives of the Platonic and Epicurean discussions, cf. C. Giussani, 'La questione del linguaggio secondo Platone e secondo Epicuro', in *Mem. R. Ist. Lombardo di Scienze e Lettere, Cl. di Lettere, Scienze storiche e morali*, 20, 1899. 3rd Ser. 11, 103–41.

32 Cf. Cicero's discussion whether words mean *natura* or *tractatione*, *Part. Or.* V.16–17; summary accounts of the debate are also given in Clem. Al. *Strom.* I.143.6; Origen, *C. Cels.* I.24 and V.45. The commonplace nature of the discussion is strongly implied in Aulus Gellius, *Noct. Att.* X.24.

both speaker and hearer. No thing or event, therefore, is a 'symbol', no expression meaningful, *nisi consensus observantis accedat* (unless the observer's agreement is given); magical invocations, to be effective, presuppose a solidarity between magician and the demons which lend magic its efficacy. 'Nor have men established conventions of using signs with determinate meanings because signs already had been meaningful (*quia iam valebant ad significationem*), but they are meaningful solely because men have in fact established the conventions for their use (*ideo valent quia consenserunt in eas*)' (II.24.37). Augustine nowhere gives any indication that he is aware of the difficulties of this position, oversimplified though it is in comparison with the subtleties of Plato's or the Epicurean treatment. He likes to escape the puzzle as to how, on his view, conventions can have been established in the first place, by invoking the biblical story of the dispersion of tongues at the Tower of Babel and their re-union in the Spirit at Pentecost; and he is, for a man of his insight, astonishingly blind to the extent that communities are created by the language they speak quite as much as they create it: that communities arise where patterns of response are shared, and that possession of a common language at once fosters and is made possible by such sharing of response-patterns. But this further insight would have involved abandoning the strict dichotomy of signs proposed in the *De doctrina Christiana*.

Expression and the word

There is no evidence that Augustine in fact abandoned this dichotomy. He never returns to it, but whether the reason for this is that he found it unsatisfactory or that it was merely of no interest in the many contexts in which he was to speak of signs throughout his work, it is impossible to say.

Although Augustine never returned to an *ex professo* treatment of signs, there are suggestions of another view of language in some of his remarks about words; and words had been taken, both in the *De magistro* and the *De doctrina Christiana*, as signs *par excellence*. In the setting of trinitarian theology, and particularly in the course of his search for created analogies in human activity and mental functioning of the ineffable Trinity, Augustine uses the notion of the 'word' as a key-concept.[33] In doing so, he is, of course, drawing on the content of a rich and complex theological tradition which cannot be outlined here. Whatever may be said about the debt of this tradition to philosophical sources, some phases of it bear the unmistakable stamp of philosophical reflection. This is true, for instance, of the use made in Christological thinking from the second century onwards of the Stoic distinction between the *logos prophorikos* (the 'word' brought forth) and the *logos endiathetos* (the 'word' placed within), a distinction which is found applied in a theological context as early as Philo. It is often very near the surface in Augustine's theological work. What, he asks, in one of his sermons on John the Baptist, is the difference between an utterance (*vox*) and a word (*verbum*)?

> A word, if it has no meaning (*rationem significantem*), is not a word. But any utterance, though it be a mere noise sounding without any meaning (*irrationabiliter perstrepat*), like the sound not of speech, but of a cry, can still be called an utterance though it cannot be said to be a word . . . It is a mere crude (*informis*) sound, which generates or induces a vibration in the ear without conveying a meaning to the understanding. A 'word', however, unless it means something, that is to say unless it conveys something to the ear and something else to the mind, is not said to be a word . . .
>
> *Sermo* 288.3 (cf. *De Trin.* XIII.1.4)

The word heard sounding outside is the sign of the word which is luminous within, which is more appropriately

33 Its use, however, is not exclusively confined to such discussions: cf. *Sermo* 288.3–4; *In Joann. Ev. tract.* 1.8 and *De cat. Rud.* 2.3.

called a 'word'. For what is brought forth by the mouth of the body is the utterance of the word (*vox verbi*); and though this, too, is called a 'word', it is so only on account of that which it is being used to manifest externally . . . That word . . . is neither brought forth in sound, nor thought in the likeness of any sound, and need not, therefore, be of any particular language; it precedes all the signs whereby it is signified and is begotten by the knowledge (*scientia*) which remains in the mind, when that knowledge is expressed (*dicitur*) as it is.

De Trin. XV.11.20

Language like this marks a profound shift of perspective: words are not now thought of as signs of things, or as standing for things; the *verbum quod foris sonat* is the sign of the *verbum quod intus lucet*, but of this latter Augustine never speaks as a sign; and yet, this is, in his view, the 'word' most properly so called. Its relation to 'words' as normally understood, to the significant sounds uttered when we speak, is left somewhat obscure. Augustine likes to take this relation as an analogy for the union of the divine Word with his human nature assumed in the Incarnation: but the analogy is scarcely illuminating, whichever way it is intended to cast its light. In general, he thinks of the word within as a complete and independent entity or event, prior to any utterance in language, and embodied in language solely for the purpose of communication. The medium in which it is embodied is a system of conventional symbols which signify the unspoken 'word' they contain, but are otherwise inessential to it. The distinction between the *verbum quod foris sonat* and the *verbum quod intus lucet* arises from the looseness of the relation between saying and meaning. We cannot conceive of our 'meaning' something without 'saying' something, yet we know that the two cannot be simply identified, for we often say what we do not mean. And yet, as Augustine's terminology itself insists, our only way of thinking of the unspoken 'word' is in terms of the ordinary words we speak and hear. We have to think away, so to speak, what we say and hear, and think of it sheerly as meaning: we have to think of a speech-word as it would be if it were not spoken or even imagined as spoken. Augustine's contention, if this picture of the movement of his dialectic is correct, is that its being embodied in speech – or any other form of 'language', gesture, for example – is inessential to what it is, though we cannot think of it except as a disembodied analogue of its embodiment.

A 'word', in this sense, is essentially meaningful and presents to the mind what it means, unlike a sign, which is meaningful only to an interpreter who knows the convention of its use. Its coming into existence is the same as its being known: 'for speaking and seeing, as external, bodily, processes, are different things; but within the mind, in thinking, the two things are the same' (*De Trin*. XV.10.18). Thus thinking is, like talking, something we do, and what we can see is what we can say; but this does not mean, as Augustine insists in asserting it, that our thoughts are not also a seeing when they are true, arising from the mind's encounter with what is given – *exortae de notitiae visionibus* (XV.10.18). The 'word' which manifests the reality known is here identical with the achieved knowledge of the reality concerned: any other 'word' would be the manifestation of something else, and no other 'word' can manifest just this reality. This 'word' is unique in each instance and has no synonyms. It is the place of the mind's encounter with the object of its experience: *res quam videndo intus dicimus* (XV.14.24). Augustine, of course, with his often tenuous hold on the sense-bound nature of our minds, did not think of this *verbum cordis* as necessarily some sensuous form or sound – or, we might add, tactual sensum, bearing in mind Helen Keller's case – created or seen as significant. He appears, on the whole, to have thought of it as a purely mental but nevertheless 'solid' product of our interior activity in thinking, which we could catch ourselves producing in the process of achieving knowledge. The knowledge achieved is the interior expression of the 'word'; but spoken utterance is merely 'putting the means furnished by the voice or by any other corporeal sign at the service of the word within' (IX.7.12), for purposes of communication. The 'word' itself is independent, not only of sound, but even of an imagined vocal schema (cf. XV.14.24; 12.22, etc.).

Augustine's theory of the 'word' approaches language from the side of the speaker, unlike the sign-theories of the *De magistro* and the *De doctrina Christiana*. The latter are theories of meaning for the spectator and the interpreter, and *prima facie* plausible only so long as we keep to that model. They do not claim to describe what the speaker or thinker is doing when he is using words or engaging in any other form of symbolising activity, however rudimentary this may be. When one is using words, images, gestures etc. in thinking and expressing what one thinks – to oneself or to others – one is not only listening to or looking at them; one is using them precisely to focus, canalise and give form to one's thinking, often in ways quite startling to oneself. There are not two separate activities here, a process we may call 'creative' and a subsequent one of 'translation', but just one process which we may call 'expressive'. Unlike the sign-theories already discussed, Augustine's theory of the 'word' recognises the 'creative' aspect of symbol-making, even though it fixes a gulf between it and its concrete embodiment. The sign-theories, though not dwelt on in this context, do not appear to be superseded, because they can be invoked to account for understanding the sensuous embodiment of the symbol. The reason for Augustine's having two theories of language, one for the *verbum vocis* (a word of the voice), approaching it from the hearer's side, and one for the *verbum mentis* approaching it from the speaker's and thinker's side, is to be sought in his bifurcation of the two *verba*. Had he thought of the *verbum mentis* as a sensuous reality endowed with meaning, or to put this in an equivalent way, of the *verbum vocis* as not a 'mere' symbol correlated with its meaning by conventional rules, then he would have been in a position to close this gap. For as the speaker can also hear the product of his own expressive activity, no special theory is required to account for what the listener does. He does the same thing as the speaker, only where the speaker creates his expressive sensuous form, the hearer has it furnished him by the speaker. It is meaningful or 'language' for him in so far as he can re-enact with its help the speaker's expressive activity embodied in it. Understanding language – if one may use this word in so wide a sense as to include all forms of expressive activity from gesture to art – is no more a matter of interpreting to oneself noises heard or shapes seen than speaking is a matter of translating into a 'language' for the benefit of others what, for oneself, has a prior non-linguistic existence.

To give anything like an adequate account of the *verbum mentis* would take us too far afield into Augustine's profoundly interesting trinitarian psychology. Such a task is still further complicated by the fact that, in his account, a 'word' is begotten by the knower from the known at every level where we can speak of 'knowledge' in any sense. Thus in tracing a trinity in the *homo exterior* (the outer man), he will detect a 'word' begotten in the encounter of sense-organ and sensum (cf. *De Trin.* XI.2.2–3; IX.11.16); again, in the generation of a *species* (form?) in the mind (*memoria*) derived from that in sense, when it attends to the latter (XI.8.13–15); and, finally, in the generation of a *species in contuitu cogitantis*, in the explicit and occurrent awareness of a thing remembered in the act of thinking (XI.9.16). At each stage of this progression inwards a 'word' is begotten in the encounter of the 'faculty of knowledge' concerned with the *species* of its object, the encounter resulting from the will's application of the activity to its object.[34]

---

34 Cf. *De Trin.* XI.8.14–15 and XI.3.6–4.7; *acies cogitantis*, as Gilson notes, seems almost to amount to a 'faculty' for Augustine. Cf. *op. cit.*, 277, n. 2.

The *verbum* 'expressed' by the mind from the *species* of the object known contained in the *memoria* and 'impressed' on this by the object – to follow Augustine's most usual way of speaking[35] – is 'true' in so far as it is a recreation in the mind's actual awareness of the *species* known in the object (cf. XV.10.17; XV.15.24). The question – to be asked time and again by Augustine's readers who confront him with an Aristotelian terminology – whether he was thinking of the process of conceiving or of judging as giving rise to the *verbum*, whether, that is to say, this is the expression of a concept or of a true judgement, does not seem to have arisen for Augustine. At the lower end of the scale, *verbum* seems to be something very like the expression of a concept; but the further we penetrate into the mind, the more we find the role of judgement predominant in Augustine's account. But it would be mistaken to identify the Aristotelian notion of judgement with the Augustinian *desuper judicium veritatis* (judgement of truth from above) (IX.6.10; cf. VIII.6.9), in the light of which images and concepts in the mind become material for its judgement. Whereas the former is essentially a logician's or epistemologist's notion, the latter is persistently close to an eschatological perspective. It is often spoken of in a way which suggests that judging involves a judgement of the mind on itself *in specie sempiternae rationis* (in the light of eternal reason) (X.2.4), on its implication with and submersion among the objects of its daily occupations – since the mind gives to its concepts and images *quiddam substantiae suae* (something of its substance) (X.5.7). The mind's judging manifests a dimension of freedom it has over its self-identification with the material images which solicit its care and threaten to engulf it. Judgement is the mind's return to itself from such 'estrangement'[36] incurred by its captivity to the sphere of its practical engagements, to the things to which 'it is

35 Cf. *ibid.*, IX.10.15–16; XI.2.3; 4.7; 8.13.
36 On this *alienatio*, see *De Trin.* XI.5.9 and *Retract.* II.15.2.

stuck by the glue of its attachments' (*curae glutino inhaeserit* – *De Trin*. X.5.7–8.11; cf. *De vera rel*. 29.52–31.58). Since, for Augustine, truth is ultimately attainable only *in ratione sempiternae veritatis* and by means of its illumination of the mind, the *verbum mentis* is above all a product of the judgement on the material presented by sense, imagination and memory in its light:

> In this eternal truth, which is the origin of all temporal things, we behold by a perception of the mind (*visu mentis*) the pattern which governs our being and our activities, whether within ourselves or in regard to other things, according to the rule of truth and of right reason; and from it we derive a true knowledge of things which we possess, as it were, in the form of a word conceived by an interior utterance . . .
>
> (*De Trin*. IX.7.12)

A great distance separates this from the superficially very similar teaching of the *De magistro*. There, words were treated as signs, that is, as sensuous things or events endowed with meaning. The role assigned to the Interior Teacher was to decipher the signs which, without the light derived from this source, would remain a mere *res*, meaningless and opaque. In the *De Trinitate*, however, the *verbum mentis* is not a sign, because it is not a sensuous reality, and Augustine does not appear to have revised his definition of signs which requires that they be perceived by sense.[37] Here the light of the eternal truth dwelling in the mind does not shine upon the 'word' as upon something opaque and meaningless without its illumination. The 'word', in so far as it is anything at all, is meaningful; this illumination is required not to confer upon the 'word' its meaning, but rather to generate a *verbum* of a thing in so far as it is discerned and evaluated in this light. The light is, so to speak, constitutive of the *verbum* begotten in it,

37 *De doctr. Christ*. II.1.2; cf. above, p. 88.

whereas the work of the Interior Teacher is confined to interpreting words already constituted, independently of his activity. Where the Teacher interprets the meaning of signs, illumination as here conceived creates the significance with which it endows its objects. Augustine would probably not have seen in his abandoning his earlier mode of speaking a change of view. No conviction had for him a compelling force comparable to that of his vision of the truth known to him as being imparted to him by God, speaking through his Scriptures or his creatures from without, and through his own mind from within. In Augustine's contemplation of this mystery words and thoughts were bound to converge in pointing towards the one ineffable source of light: what mattered to him is what they were pointing at, even if they happened to be pointing there from many different places and directions. He is much more concerned with the Interior Teacher dwelling in the mind and teaching within, than with the external signs which he deciphers for us; and he is much more interested in his identity with the Word 'whose participation is our illumination, the Word who is the life which is the light of men' (*De Trin*. IV.2.4), than he is in the difference between the signs and words interpreted by the one and the 'words' begotten in the light of the other.

APPENDIX: NOTE ON TERMINOLOGY

The correlations of terminology noted here are given merely to avoid some of the opportunities for misunderstanding. No adequate correlation can be provided without at least some account of the theories of meaning of which the terminology forms a part.

1: Sign (Representamen) – Object – Subject (Interpretant): This is Peirce's terminology, and it coincides closely with Augustine's. Peirce's definition of 'sign' is equally close to that given by Augustine: 'A sign or representamen is something which stands to somebody for something in some respect or capacity' (Buchler, *The Philosophy of Peirce* (London, 1940) 99). Modern definitions known to me are all variants of this.

2: Symbol: Peirce distinguishes, in the second of his three trichotomies of signs ('according as the relation of the sign to its object consists in the sign having some character in itself, or in some existential relation to its object, or in its relation to an interpretant' – *ibid.*, 101), what he calls 'icons', 'indexes' and 'symbols'. A 'symbol' in his terminology denotes roughly the same sort of sign as Augustine's *signa data*: 'A symbol is a sign which refers to an object that it denotes by virtue of a law, usually an association of general ideas, which operates to cause the symbol to be interpreted as referring to that object' (*ibid.*, 102). Similar, though more narrowly restricted, is the sense given to 'symbol' by Collingwood; on the other hand, he regards symbolism as only one element in expressive language, one which arises as a result of its progressive 'intellectualisation' (*The Principles of Art* (Oxford, 1938) Ch. XI). A still more restricted sense is assigned to 'symbol' by Professor Ryle such that signs like ⊃ for 'implies', √ for 'square root of' etc. are typical examples of symbols (cf. the symposium on *Thinking and Language, Arist. Soc. Suppl.* XXV (1951) 71– 72). Professor Price distinguishes from this restricted sense of 'symbol' an extended sense which he allows as legitimate. This latter includes words, phrases, sentences, gestures, diagrams, etc. (*Thinking and experience* (London, 1953) 143–47). Symbols are defined in a similar sense by Susan Stebbing as 'a sign consciously designed to stand for something' (*A Modern Introduction to Logic* (London, 1930) 11). Her further division of these into 'natural' and 'conventional' does not concern us, except to note that the former do not correspond to Augustine's *signa naturalia*, but would be a sub-class of his *signa data*. The distinction has been severely, and I think rightly criticised by Price (*op. cit.*, Ch. VI). For Mrs Langer, a 'symbol' includes all the wider meaning which, following

Collingwood, I have sometimes spoken of as 'expressive' form. ('Symbols are not proxy for their objects, but are vehicles for the conception of objects' – *Philosophy in a New Key*, 2nd ed. (Oxford, 1951) 60–61). Augustine's definition of *signa data* seems to be intended for 'symbols' in this wide sense; but his account of meaning by convention seems in effect to restrict them to the kinds of sign referred to as 'symbols' by Ryle and Collingwood, and distinguished as 'symbols' in a narrower sense by Price. Masure notes the fluidity of meaning and overtones associated with the words 'sign' and 'symbol' (*op. cit.*, 18).

3: Symptom: This corresponds fairly accurately to Peirce's 'index', which he defines as a sign 'which refers to the object it denotes by virtue of being really affected by that object' (*loc. cit.*, 102). This is the sense which Price gives to 'sign', which he contrasts with 'symbol' (*op. cit.*, chapters IV–V). This is also equivalent to Mrs Langer's usage of 'sign' (*op. cit.*, 57), though, following a usage of Charles Morris, she suggests in her Preface to the second edition 'signal' as an alternative, precisely with the intention to leave 'sign' free to mean, as in Augustine's and Peirce's terminology, 'any vehicle of meaning, signal or symbol . . .' (*op. cit.*, viii). She restricts 'symptom' to mean a sign (signal) which is part of the total condition which it signifies (*op. cit.*, 57, n. 4).

4: An 'Icon', for Peirce, 'is a sign which refers to the object that it denotes merely by virtue of characters of its own . . .' (*loc. cit.*, 102). A good case could, I think, be made out in favour of Augustine's dichotomy as against Peirce's trichotomy; but we must merely note here that for Augustine any sign must have *similitudo* in some sense to its object; but as the *similitudo* required is so vague and of such diverse types, it is not, as he notes, sufficient to constitute a foundation for a sign-relation, but requires, in addition, one or other of the relations to object or subject for 'significance' (cf. *De doctr. Christ.* II.25.38). It should be noted, however, that for Peirce, too, some sort of

Icon is involved in every Index and some sort of Index in every Symbol.

A similitudo of special importance for Augustine may be noted here, which he calls *imago* (and *vestigium*: how these two are distinguished is not relevant here – cf. *De Trin.* VI.10.11; IX.11.16; XI.1.1). This is a *similitudo* which, in addition to likeness, involves some form of existential dependence on an original. Thus, for instance, the reflection of a face in a mirror is an *imago* of the face, but not *vice versa*, although the likeness holds both ways (*De div. quaest. LXXXIII*, 74). This relation of dependence would make *imago* and *vestigium* classifiable under the heading of *signa naturalia*.

Chapter Four
SIGNS, COMMUNICATION
AND COMMUNITIES
IN AUGUSTINE'S
DE DOCTRINA CHRISTIANA

Hier ist des Säglichen Zeit, hier ist Heimat.   Rilke

The explosion of semiotics during the second half of our century has not left the study of ancient Christian literature untouched; and no work has been more directly exposed to the blast than the *De doctrina Christiana*.[1] Indeed, it might even be held to have contributed to the force of the explosion; for Augustine's discussion of signs has been described as the first to merit the name of 'semiotics', its originality consisting in its success in rounding off the achievements of classical antiquity in a new synthesis.[2] Augustine is widely said to be the first to have integrated the theory of language – 'fifteen centuries before De Saussure'[3] – into that of the sign. Of this very large subject my paper will be concerned with only one corner: the sign as a means of communication, and the way

1 See Appendix for Select Bibliography. References in the sequel are given by name and (date). References to works not listed there are given in full.
2 See Todorov (1977), 55–56; 179; and n. 3 below.
3 Eco (1984), 33; cf. Simone (1972) 9–10, 29–30, and Handelman (1982) 107–20. I concluded this in my study, 'St Augustine on signs' (1957). My argument (and that of subsequent writers who have accepted it) on Augustine's originality needs to be qualified in the light of Jackson (1969) and Duchrow (1965) 50–51.

that the notions of sign and communication opened a way for Augustine to speak of communities.

'Community' in some sense is a necessary condition of any communication – a 'community' of understanding, whether it be of gesture, words or other significant acts. Augustine was clearly conscious of this in defining and classifying *signa*. I begin with a summary of these definitions and the classification.

Signs

In the *De doctrina Christiana* Augustine defines signs twice over:

(i) signs are 'things which are used to signify something' (*res . . . quae ad significandum aliquid adhibentur* – I.2.2): the relationship is between the sign-thing, its user, and that which he uses it to signify. Similarly in the second, slightly more elaborate, definition Augustine gives a little later:

(ii) 'A sign is a thing which causes us to think of something in addition to the impression it makes upon the senses' (*res praeter speciem quam ingerit sensibus aliud alquid ex se faciens in cogitationem uenire* – II.1.1): here the relationship is between the sign-thing, its perceiver (for the present purpose this is the chief difference from (i), which refers to the sign-user), and that further thing which it brings to its perceiver's mind, the signified.

Of the three terms in Augustine's two definitions two are constant: the sign and the signified. The third term differs, according to the different points of view from which the two definitions are given: the first from the point of view of the sign-giver (or user); the second from that of the sign-receiver (or perceiver). The reason why his more elaborate definition is given from the point of view of the sign-receiver rather than from that of the sign-giver becomes clear from the classification of signs which immediately follows this second definition: for not all signs are *given*, though all – because a thing is a sign in so far as it stands for something to somebody; to be a sign, a thing must necessarily be experienced by some subject – are received.

We must now look at this division of *signa* into the two great classes distinguished by Augustine:

(i) *signa naturalia*, which Augustine defines as those which 'from themselves make known something other than themselves without any wish or desire on anybody's part of signifying; as, for instance, smoke signifies fire' (*quae sine uoluntate atque ullo appetitu significandi praeter se aliquid aliud ex se cognosci faciunt . . . –* II.1.2). The second class is that of

(ii) *signa data*, given signs, those which 'living beings give to one another in order to indicate, as far as they can, their feelings, their perceptions or their thoughts' (*quae sibi quaeque uiuentia inuicem dant ad demonstrandos, quantum possunt, motus animi sui, uel sensa aut intellecta quaelibet –* II.2.3, a little freely translated).

The first class, that of 'natural signs', thus comprises those which stand for something in virtue of their link – by causal dependence, logical implication, being a syndrome – with that which they signify. The second is the class of those which signify in virtue of their givers' intention. The sign, to be a sign, in all cases has a relation to two other terms: the signified, and the giver or perceiver; which of the two classes it falls into will, however, be determined by whether it depends on the giver or on the signified. Both the definitions given in the *De doctrina Christiana* are, in other words, triadic, though this triadic relation presupposes a (dyadic) relation of dependence between the sign and either the signified or the giver/perceiver.[4]

4 Markus (1957) 73–74, endorsed by Jackson (1969) 96. See also Jordan (1980) 184. Similarly, Bouchard (1980) 343–44, on the *De dialectica*. This is obscured in much modern semiotic writing, e.g. Eco (1984), though he mentions Peirce's three-term definition (14) and writes (46) that 'a Sign is not only something which stands for something else; it is also something that can

Intentional, 'given', signs result from acts of communication: as Augustine observes, the only reason for signifying, that is, for giving signs (*significandi, id est signi dandi*), is to bring forth (*ad depromendum*) what is going on in the mind of the sign-giver and to communicate it (*ad traiciendum*) to another's mind (II.2.3). We need not go into the philosophical problems of what it is that is being communicated in such acts of communication;[5] what is important for our discussion is Augustine's view on the way the sign receives its meaning. Augustine appears to resolve the ancient debate about whether signs have their significance by nature or by convention by distinguishing among 'given signs' some, such as, apparently, signs made by animals to warn of danger and the like, which signify by nature, from others, such as letters of the various alphabets and words (spoken or written), which signify by convention.[6]

Most (though not necessarily all) 'given signs', Augustine evidently thought, have their meanings conferred on them by convention.[7] Convention, however, is a notion with a more complex sense than Augustine's statements sometimes suggest. This is clearest when we examine what he has to say about those signs through which human beings communicate

---

and must be interpreted', and in fact generally speaks of the sign in terms of a relation between two terms. I avoid the terminology of 'signifier' and 'signified', and use Augustine's 'sign' and 'signified'. Kirwan (1989) 38 argues (unconvincingly) that Augustine's definition fails to take into account undetected signs.

5 The best discussions are Jackson (1969) 107–11 and O'Daly (1987) 175–78. See also Kirwan (1989) 39–40.

6 *De doctr. Christ.* II.24.37. See Jackson (1969) 97–98 for details. For a discussion of the historical significance of this view of language, see Milbank (1988).

7 In my paper (Markus (1957) 74–76), I called 'given' signs 'conventional'. Jackson (1969) 97, rightly remarks that this is going beyond what Augustine is asserting in these chapters. Similarly Engels (1962) who argues that they are to be described as 'intentional'. I have adopted this terminology.

with demons in magical and other 'superstitious' practices (on which see below, pp. 125–46). All these rest on 'pacts about certain meanings agreed with demons by contract' (*pacta quaedam significationum cum daemonibus placita atque foederata* – II.20.30). The idea of such an agreement is at first sight puzzling. But Augustine insists on it repeatedly, in language of almost legal precision.[8] He leaves us in no doubt that he thought of the agreed symbolic system as the bond of association: 'these arts of idle and noxious superstition [are] constituted by a certain association through faithless and deceitful friendship (*pacta infidelis et dolosae amicitiae*)' (II.23.36); 'they [omens, auguries etc.] are valid only to the extent that they have been established by presumptuous minds as a common language agreed with demons (*tantum ualent, quantum praesumptione animorum quasi communi quadam lingua cum daemonibus foederata sunt*)' (II.24.37). Like words,

> all these meanings are understood according to the conventions of the society, and, as these conventions differ, are understood differently; nor are they agreed upon among men because they already had a meaning, but they receive their meaning from the agreement (*hae omnes significationes pro suae cuiusque societatis consensione animos mouent et, quia diuersa consensio est, diuerse mouent, nec ideo consenserunt in eas homines, quia iam ualebant ad significationem, sed ideo ualent quia consenserunt in eas* – II.24.37).

But, of course, magicians and soothsayers do not make an agreement with demons and then go on to use the conventions agreed on. It must be the intention to enter such an association that lies at the roots of the conventions which hold it together. It is as if a person entered the 'contract' with the demons in the very movement of his will towards the demons with whom he

8 *De doctr. Christ.* II.20.30; 22.34; 23.36; 24.37; 25.38; 39.58.

associates himself. In this these signs are like all 'given', intentional, signs: they are 'the kind of thing which starts a motion towards what it signifies and, mediately, towards whomever employs it as a sign'.[9]

Communication

Communication is a necessary condition for community; but direct communication between human minds, a transparency of mutual understanding, is not possible in the fallen human condition.[10] Language arises from the conflict of this impossibility with the natural human need for community: 'there could be no solid association between men unless they could communicate (*nisi colloquerentur*), and unless they could thus share, as it were, their minds and their thoughts (*sibi mentes suas et cogitationes quasi refunderent*)'; for this reason, 'that which is rational in us . . . and is drawn into association by a kind of natural bond with those with whom it shares its rationality . . . has imposed words, that is to say, certain meaningful sounds, upon things.'[11] Language bridges the gulf that has opened up between fallen human beings; but words are fragile vehicles of meaning, they slip, slide and will not stay still, and every attempt to communicate is a wholly new start, for, as Augustine wrote, 'understanding flashes like lightning through the mind, but speech is slow and sluggish, and hopelessly inadequate (*locutio tarda et longa est, longeque dissimilis*)'.[12]

9 Jordan (1980) 186.

10 *De Gen. c. Man.* II.4.5; it will be restored in the risen body: *patebunt etiam cogitationes nostrae inuicem nobis* (*Dc Ciu. Dei* XXII.29.6). Cf. Mayer (1969) 355, with further references. Cf. also Beierwaltes (1971) 185 on word as communication, with references in n. 17; Louth (1989) 156–57 and, especially, Duchrow (1961).

11 *De ord.* II.12.35. Cf. Kuypers (1934) 60 on man's social nature as based on semantic activity.

12 *De cat. rud.* 2.3.

For Augustine semantic activity – understanding and communicating through language – was the index of the human
need for transcendence in the most general terms: for union
with other minds in the very act of understanding a shared
world. Take the occurrence in conversation of a word whose
meaning is unknown: what is the nature of the frustration it
causes, what is the object of the urge to clear up its meaning?
Augustine's answer is most fully given in a richly dense
chapter of the *De Trinitate* (X.1.2). Here he argues that,
assuming the unknown word to be a sign, i.e., to have
meaning, we will have the urge to discover that meaning, to
free ourselves from confinement within a wall of opaque signs.
'Knowing it to be a sign and not a mere brute noise, he will
wish to know it perfectly', and thus to know its meaning. The
driving force is what Augustine calls 'love'; the term which
includes what we should call urges, desires, passions, setting a
value upon things. The distinction he makes at the beginning
of the *De doctrina Christiana* (I.3.3) between two modes of
loving, *frui* and *uti*, 'enjoying' and 'using', or loving (desiring,
setting a value on) something either for itself or for the sake of
something else,[13] is crucial to the theory of signs and meaning
to which the second Book is devoted. For, as Rowan Williams
has shown in an impressive study,[14] 'it is the means whereby
Augustine links what he has to say about language with what
he has to say about beings who "mean" and about the
fundamentally desirous nature of those beings – a link which is
undoubtedly the most original and interesting feature of the
treatise'. To 'enjoy' something that is less than the ultimate,
infinite satisfaction, that is to say to allow the will to rest in its
possession; or to wish to 'enjoy' it, that is to say, to limit

13 The classic discussion of this is Lorenz (1952/53); see also the
important study by O. O'Donovan, '*Usus* and *fruitio* in Augustine, *De
doctrina Christiana* I', *JThS* n.s. 33 (1982) 361–97.

14 Williams (1989). The quotation is from p. 139. I owe much to this
paper, especially in this section.

desire to its attainment, without pointing to a further horizon, is a perversion of the natural and rational order of willing. To allow desire to cease in this way is premature closure of the Christian life, a denial of the restlessness in the depth of the human heart.

This is Augustine's way of affirming the necessity of keeping our horizons perpetually open, of seeking meaning in things experienced as signs, and to be inclined to suspect that what is not so experienced ought to be. We thwart this drive of our nature only at the cost of blocking off the process of learning and growth that living in the midst of this realm of limited and unstable things ought always to remain. A tendency to discover things to be signs is central to Augustine's understanding of what it is to be human, and (as we shall see below, p. 116) doubly so to his idea of being Christian. It is hardly surprising to find that this understanding is also the foundation of his view on the meanings of scriptural symbols, of the Old Testament,[15] and of the created world as a whole.[16] These, however, are large themes I cannot go into here. I keep here to the most fundamental point, the understanding of signs itself. What is it that makes us want to understand meaning? What is it we are engaged in when we try to penetrate the obscurity of an unknown sign, to refuse to be confined within opacity?

Augustine's answer as it is worked out in this chapter of the *De Trinitate* – the fullest he gives anywhere, so far as I know, and deeply Platonic in its inspiration – is formulated in terms of 'love'. What is it that is loved in the search for meaning launched by the frustration of hearing a word not understood? Nothing can be loved that is not known; so the object of desire cannot be the unknown object referred to; nor, evidently, is it

15 See especially Jordan (1980) 189–91.

16 On this, see especially Mayer (1974) 'Significationshermeneutik'; his other studies listed in the Select Bibliography give a fine account of the uses to which Augustine put his theory of signs.

the opaque sign itself, nor the known fact that it has *a* meaning. So what is the object of the desire that urges one to seek understanding?

> What else is it but the knowledge and the awareness in the principles of things (*in rationibus rerum*) of the beauty of the knowledge (*pulchritudo doctrinae*) which reveals the meaning of all signs, and of the value of that skill (*peritia*) by which men communicate with one another in their societies? Only thus can human groups avoid being worse, through inability to share their thoughts by communicating, than any kind of solitariness. (*ibid.*)

This beauty and this usefulness, Augustine concludes, is what the soul loves in seeking meanings: the search for meaning is the quest for transcendence – transcendence of the self imprisoned among opaque signs, isolated from the linguistic community no less than from the realm of meanings. Escape from this isolation is what 'he who seeks the meaning of unknown significant sounds seeks to realise within himself'. He will have to limit his studies to what he has hope of achieving; in principle, however, the whole world of meanings challenges him to pursue, 'burning with fervent longing (*ferventius amore inardescit*)', an understanding in which opacity will disclose its meaning.

> He who seeks [the meaning of an unknown word] is in the grip of a quest for discovery (*in studio discendi*) and would seem to love something unknown; but in reality this is not the case. For his soul is touched by that idea (*species*) which he knows and is aware of, in which the value of an association of minds communicating in the hearing and the uttering of understood words is made apparent (*in qua elucet decus consociandorum animorum uocibus notis audiendis atque reddendis*); this is what kindles the ardour of one seeking to understand what he does not know, aware though he is of a known form

> (*notam formam*) to which it refers, which is the object of
> his love . . . For nearly all rational souls are prone to see
> the beauty of this skill, by which the objects thought
> among men are known through the enunciation of
> meaningful sounds. (*ibid*.)[17]

So in learning the meaning of signs we discover a shared world
and are simultaneously integrated into our linguistic community. Integration in the linguistic community *is* discovery of
meaning, and, conversely, the search for meaning heals
ruptures in the linguistic community. These are the two sides
of the liberation from captivity to the sign. To seek meaning is
to enact transcendence.

   Augustine expounds this most fully in the *De Trinitate*, in
the context of his investigation of the love which impels the
human soul to recognise itself as the image of the triune God.
The same conception is succinctly expounded in the *De
doctrina Christiana* (especially II.8.12–9.13). Here, although
his objectives are more limited, the recognition that 'language
in its fluidity and displacements is inseparably interwoven
with the restlessness or openness of desire that is what is
fundamentally human'[18] underlies, and gives unity to, the
whole discussion of the *De doctrina Christiana*.

Communities

Augustine knew perfectly well how hard we find it to learn
foreign languages; and in the chapter of the *De Trinitate* we
have just been considering, he recognises the natural desire to
expand our linguistic equipment to infinity, but makes gener-

17 See the commentary on this passage by O'Daly (1987) 209. Cf.
Duchrow (1965) 119–20, commenting on this chapter of the *De Trinitate*
and comparing its more positive perspective (made possible by the stress on
the role of love) with that of *Conf*. I.7–13.
18 Williams (1989) 148, and the fine study of Jordan (1980) especially
194–96 on the 'dialectical' character of signs.

ous concession to our need to restrict it to the sphere within which we have some hope of attaining our objective. In fact, our many separate languages will always restrict us to moving within a limited variety of linguistic communities, and will therefore limit the boundaries of attainable meaning for us in a variety of ways. If in the *De Trinitate* Augustine is more interested in the furthest reach of the potential for transcendence, in the *De doctrina Christiana* he is more concerned to explore limited human communities. Book II of the work is nothing less – though it may be rather more – than an account of how communities are constituted by the way they understand the symbolic systems (i.e. all that Augustine includes under his category of *signa data*) in use within them.

A particular human group is defined by the boundaries of the system of signs in use among its members. This is the consequence of Augustine's theory of signs. Signs must mean something to somebody; the somebodies who agree on their meaning will constitute a (linguistic) community. The triadic relation of signification is the key to Augustine's entire hermeneutic theory. A sign is a 'thing' standing within the signifying relation between a subject, the sign-thing itself, and the signified object. The latter in its turn can be, or become, a sign when drawn into a further relationship of signification (see above, pp. 10–11). Thus many signs may have meanings on two levels. Transferred (or 'figurative', as they are generally described) signs are, in Augustine's definition, quite simply signs whose signifieds are placed into a second relationship of signification: they occur when 'the things signified by their proper literal names (*propriis uerbis*) are in their turn used to signify something else' (II.10.15).[19] Augustine gives the exam-

19 This is, of course, the position widely adopted by modern theories of metaphor, e.g. in P. Ricoeur, *The rule of metaphor: multi-disciplinary studies of the creation of meaning in language* (E. trans. London, 1978) quoting (188) P. Henle, 'Metaphor', in *Language, thought, and culture*, ed. P. Henle (Ann Arbor, 1958): 'the word is "an immediate sign of its literal sense and a mediate sign of its figurative sense" ' quoted from p. 175.

ple of the word 'ox', used literally to signify the beast normally designated by the word; in its figurative sense it will signify the evangelist to those familiar with the scriptural discourse within which the beast itself can stand for the evangelist.[20] Hence the importance which Augustine attaches (II.16.24) to the exegete being at home within the relevant secular discourses: how can he appreciate the scriptural symbolism of the serpent if he doesn't know what snakes really are like? This possibility of meaning on two levels gives rise to a language constituting linguistic communities on two levels. We might say that someone who understands the word 'ox' belongs to a primary linguistic community (e.g. of English speakers), whereas someone who understands what its signified (the ox) can mean in a further (e.g. scriptural) context belongs, in addition, to a secondary linguistic community.

What distinguishes the Christian from the Jewish community is such an openness to the New Testament context within which the things spoken of in the Old Testament receive a further meaning. Lack of it is the 'servitude' of the Jewish people, the closure of their biblical discourse short of the new realm of meaning it would enter in the light of the Incarnation (III.5.9–6.10); and it is from this servitude to the sign that 'Christian freedom has liberated those it found in subjection to useful signs . . . by raising them, through interpreting the signs to which they were subject, to the things of which those signs were the signs' (III.8.12). Captivity to the sign is

---

Cf. P. Ricoeur, *Time and narrative* (Chicago, 1984) x–xi for a good summary of Ricoeur's views. On scriptural hermeneutics and allegory, see his *Essays on biblical interpretation*, ed. L. S. Mudge (London, 1981) 51–53: 'Scripture appears here [in medieval *lectio divina*] as an inexhaustible treasure which stimulates thought about everything, which conceals a total interpretation of the world. . . Hermeneutics is the very deciphering of life in the mirror of the text. . .'

20 The same distinction is made in *De doctrina Christiana* I.2.2: on scriptural *res* which are 'things in such a manner that they are also signs of other things'.

inability, or refusal, to pierce its opacity; not knowing, or not seeking, the range of potential further meaning it can have in a larger discourse (III.9.13).

The Jews who refused to understand the Old Testament as interpreted in the New thus remained captive to the closed world of its 'useful' signs. As so often in Augustine's thought, this patristic commonplace becomes part of a deeply thought-out general view with much wider bearings. The theory of signs and meaning in terms of which it is worked out also provides his means for defining other communities within the overall human community. The *De doctrina Christiana* is the work in which he first undertook the task – to which he returned on a grand scale in *The City of God* – of defining the identity of the Christian community within the context of the institutions – the 'culture', as we might not inappropriately say – of the secular world in which it is set.

The *De doctrina Christiana* can be read as exploring the place of a Christian sub-culture within the literary culture shared among the educated Roman public. Augustine is here at grips with questions about 'the function of effects of specialised forms of language in the life of the religious community, of how this affects the way in which a community is perceived from the outside, and, not least, of how it is possible for individuals to be bilingual and bicultural – like Augustine – in this respect'.[21] Augustine expounds his notion of a community constituted by its symbolic systems in what he has to say about the *instituta* of human beings. Human *instituta* are one of the two sectors into which he divides knowledge: it is either of things instituted by human beings themselves, or of the things they have discovered and observed in what has been instituted by God (II.19.29): 'nature' and 'culture', as we might roughly label them. It is 'culture' we must explore here; as Augustine's discussion indicates, it includes such things as languages, arts, sciences and disci-

21 Williams (1989) 138.

plines, as well as customs and rites carried out within a society. This human 'culture' Augustine divides into two sorts: that which is superstitious, and that which is not. I start with the first and then go on to the non-superstitious.

The idolatrous, magical, divinatory, or astrological practices Augustine groups together under the heading of 'superstitious practices' are enumerated in five paragraphs (II.20.30–22.34). The class comprises practices (*quicquid institutum est ab hominibus*) that pertain to the making and worshipping of idols, or to the worship of creatures, or parts of creatures, as divine, or to consultation and 'pacts about certain meanings agreed with demons by contract' (II.20.30).[22] In these superstitious practices the demons, Augustine tells us, are parties to the agreement which established the conventions. The very language that constitutes this community is inherently demonic. But words can belong to more than one language. There is a hint, for instance, that some practices can be ambiguous: hanging certain objects on one's body, for instance, or taking certain foods or drinks, might be either sinister acts of superstition, or sensible medication (II.20.30; cf. 29.45). Augustine seems to treat such signs as capable of belonging to two different languages: either to one resting on demonic convention, or to another resting on human convention. This element of polysemy takes us into the second branch of his division of human *instituta*.

This is the class of human institutions which are not superstitious, 'that is to say, instituted not with demons, but [only] among men themselves' (II.25.38). Augustine further sub-divides these into a class containing those *instituta* which are 'useful and necessary' (*commoda et necessaria*) and a class of those which are 'superfluous and extravagant' (*superflua et luxuriosa* – II.25.38). In the *De doctrina Christiana* Augustine is interested in the part of the secular culture that is 'useful and necessary' to a Christian, and therefore he does not go to any

22 On these 'pacts', see above, p. 109.

trouble to specify what, apart from fictitious fables and falsehoods, he would include among the 'superfluous and extravagant', though he allows us to guess that he would, at any rate, include the pleasures of the theatre and the like.[23] We should note a significant difference between the way Augustine deals with such institutions and the way they are treated in a tradition of patristic rhetoric well established since Tertullian, for whom they were nothing short of demonic: 'every monument [of the circus] is a temple'.[24] 'By this shall they know a man for a Christian', Tertullian wrote, 'that he has repudiated the shows.'[25] For Augustine, a frequenter of the shows would, at worst, have counted as a depraved pleasure-seeker, not an idolater. But the institutions he is interested in here are the useful and necessary: those, like the conventions of dress, weights and measures, and the innumerable kinds of symbolism (*innumerabilia genera significationum*), which are useful and necessary to the smooth functioning of human societies (*sine quibus humana societas aut non omnino aut minus commode geritur* – II.25.39). Such institutions and symbols helped to secure the cohesion of civil society, and were to be valued on that account. Christians should be encouraged to pursue secular disciplines, 'soberly and critically', that is to say under no illusion that they are capable of bringing salvation; they must avoid those which imply association with the demonic realm, and should abstain from those that are superfluous and luxurious; but they must not neglect 'those institutions which are of value to human beings living

23 I have argued in my *The end of ancient Christianity* (Cambridge, 1990) 110–23, that Augustine would not have included among the 'superfluous and extravagant' some of the *spectacula*, such as the circus races, before April 399; information recently come to light may suggest that Augustine did not abandon his earlier views until as late as 407–08. On the recently discovered letters, see F. Dolbeau, 'Sermons inédits de S. Augustin dans un manuscrit de Mayence (Stadtbibliothek I 9)', *REAug* 36 (1990) 355–59.

24 *De spect.* 8.3. On this subject, see my *The end of ancient Christianity*, 101–02, 120–21.

25 . . . *de repudio spectaculorum*: *De spect.* 24.3.

together in groups (*quae ad societatem conuiuentium ualent*) in the pursuit of the needs of this life' (II.39.58; cf. 25.40).

Here is that vivid sense of the importance of appreciating and fostering secular institutions catering for the cohesion of a mixed society which Augustine will explore far more fully in the *City of God*. There it is formulated in terms of the intermediate goods which are to be valued by members of both the earthly and the heavenly Cities.[26] In the *De doctrina Christiana* Augustine is more concerned with the possibilities of a shared culture. The terms in which he explores the relationships of groups sharing a culture, or of sub-cultures within a society, are those of a hermeneutic of symbolic systems. In the *De doctrina Christiana* Augustine has devised a sophisticated and powerful conceptual scheme for discussing the whole realm of human culture and activity which he had once summed up as *magna haec et omnino humana* (*De quant. an.* 33.72): these great, and wholly human, achievements.[27]

SELECT BIBLIOGRAPHY

1: General works with some discussion of Augustine's theory of signs

Todorov, T., *Théories du symbole* (Paris, 1977)

Handelman, S. A., *The slayers of Moses: the emergence of Rabbinic interpretation in modern literary theory* (Albany, N.Y., 1982)

Colish, M. L., *The mirror of language. A study in medieval theory of knowledge* (Lincoln, Nebr., 2nd ed. 1983)

Eco, U., *Semiotics and the philosophy of language* (London, 1984)

Vance, E., *Mervelous signals: Poetics and sign theory in the Middle Ages* (Lincoln, Nebr., 1986)

26 See my *Saeculum: History and society in the theology of Saint Augustine* (Cambridge, 2nd ed. 1988) 45–71.

27 I wish to thank Gerard O'Daly for most helpful comments.

O'Daly, G. P., *Augustine's philosophy of mind* (London, 1987)

Milbank, J., 'Theology without substance: Christianity, signs, origins', *Literature and theology* 2 (1988) 1–17 & 33–52

Kirwan, C., *Augustine* (The arguments of the philosophers. London, 1989) 35–59

Rist, J. M., *Augustine. Ancient thought baptized* (Cambridge, 1994)

Irvine, M., *The making of textual culture* (Cambridge, 1994)

2: Discussions of Augustine's theory of signs

Three studies (marked *) not concerned with the *De doctrina christiana* are included for their relevance.

Kuypers, K., *Der Zeichen- und Wortbegriff im Denken Augustins* (Amsterdam, 1934)

Markus, R. A., 'Saint Augustine on signs', *Phronesis* 2 (1957) 60–83 (also in *Augustine: a collection of critical studies*, ed. R. A. Markus (New York, 1972) 61–91; references given with this pagination)

Duchrow, U., '«Signum» und «superbia» beim jungen Augustin (386–390)', *REAug* 7 (1961) 369–72

Engels, J., 'La doctrine du signe chez saint Augustin', *StPatr* 6 (*TU* 81, 1962) 366–73

*Pinborg, J., 'Das Sprachdenken der Stoa und Augustins Dialektik', *Classica et medievalia* 23 (1962) 148–77

*Holl, A., *Die Welt der Zeichen bei Augustin. Religionsphänomenologische Analyse des 13. Buches der Confessiones* (Wien, 1963)

Duchrow, U., *Sprachverständnis und biblisches Hören bei Augustin* (Tübingen, 1965)

Jackson, B. D., 'The theory of signs in St Augustine's *De doctrina Christiana*', *REAug* 15 (1969) 9–49 (also in *Augustine: a collection of critical studies*, ed. R. A. Markus (New York, 1972) 92–147; references given with this pagination)

Mayer, C. P., *Die Zeichen in der geistigen Entwicklung und in der Theologie des jungen Augustinus* (Cassiciacum, 24/1. Würzburg, 1969)

Beierwaltes, W., 'Zu Augustins Metaphysik der Sprache', *AugSt* 2 (1971) 179–95

Simone, R., 'Sémiologie augustinienne', *Semiotica* 6 (1972) 1–31

Mayer, C. P., *Die Zeichen in der geistigen Entwicklung und in der Theologie Augustinus*: II. Teil: *Die antimanichäische Epoche* (Cassiciacum, 24/2. Würzburg, 1974)

Allard, G. H., 'L'articulation du sens et du signe dans le «De doctrina Christiana» de s. Augustin', *StPatr* 14 (*TU* 117, Berlin, 1976) 377–88

*Daniels, D. E., 'The argument of the *De Trinitate* and Augustine's theory of signs', *AugSt* 8 (1977) 33–54

Bouchard, G., 'La conception augustinienne du signe selon Tzvetan Todorov', *RechAug* 15 (1980) 305–46

Baratin, M., 'Les origines stoïciennes de la théorie augustinienne du signe', *REL* 59 (1981) 260–68

Bernard, R. W., *In Figura: Terminology pertaining to figurative exegesis in the works of Augustine of Hippo* (Unpublished Dissertation; Princeton, 1984)

Todorov, T., 'A propos de la conception augustinienne du signe', *REAug* 31 (1985) 209–14

Louth, A., 'Augustine on language', *Literature and theology* 3 (1989) 151–68

Burnyeat, M., 'Wittgenstein and Augustine *De magistro*', *Aristotelian Society. Supplementary volume* 61 (1987) 1–24

Pollmann, K., *Doctrina Christiana. Untersuchungen zu den Anfängen der christlichen Hermeneutik von Augustinus, De doctrina Christiana* (Habilitationsschrift. Konstanz, 1995)

3: Other discussions of *De doctrina Christiana*: purpose, public, structure and argument

Brunner, P., 'Charismatische und methodische Schriftauslegung nach Augustins Prolog zu «De doctrina Christiana»', *Kerygma und Dogma* 1 (1955) 59–69, 85–103

Hill, E., 'De doctrina Christiana: a suggestion', *StPatr* 6 (*TU* 81, 1962) 443–46

Martin, J., 'Abfassung, Veröffentlichung und Überlieferung von Augustins Schrift «De doctrina Christiana»', *Traditio* 18 (1962) 69–87

Duchrow, U., 'Zum Prolog von Augustins *De doctrina Christiana*', *VigChr* 17 (1963) 165–72

Kevane, E., 'Paideia and anti-paideia: the Proemium of St Augustine's «De doctrina Christiana»', *AugSt* 1 (1970) 153–80

Verheijen, L. M. J., 'Le *De doctrina Christiana* de saint Augustin. Un manuel d'herméneutique et d'expression chrétienne avec, en II.19.29–42.63, une «charte fondamentale pour une culture chrétienne»', *Augustiniana* 24 (1974) 10–20

Mayer, C. P., '«Res per signa»: Der Grundgedanke des Prologs in Augustins Schrift *De doctrina Christiana* und das Problem seiner Datierung', *REAug* 20 (1974) 100–12

Mayer, C. P., 'Significationshermeneutik im Dienst der Daseinsauslegung – Die Funktion der Verweisung in den *Confessiones* X–XIII', *Augustiniana* 24 (1974) 21–74

Sieben, H.-J., 'Die «res» der Bibel. Eine Analyse von Augustinus, *De doctrina Christiana* I–III', *REAug* 21 (1975) 72–90

Jordan, M. D., 'Words and word: Incarnation and signification in Augustine's *De doctrina Christiana*', *AugSt* 11 (1980) 177–96

Press, G. A., 'The subject and structure of Augustine's *De doctrina Christiana*', *AugSt* 11 (1980) 99–124

O'Donovan, O., '*Usus* and *fruitio* in Augustine, *De doctrina Christiana* I', *JThS* n.s. 33 (1982) 361–97

Moreau, M., 'Lecture du «De doctrina Christiana»', *Saint Augustin et la Bible*, ed. A.-M. La Bonnardière (*Bible de tous les temps*, 3. Paris, 1986) 253–85

Poland, L. M., 'Augustine, allegory, and conversion', *Literature and theology* 2 (1988) 37–48

Williams, R. D., 'Language, reality and desire in Augustine's *De doctrina*', *Literature and theology* 3 (1989) 138–50

Alici, L., *S. Agostino d'Ippona: La dottrina Cristiana* (Milano, 1989)

The classic studies of great importance which touch on the theme and should be included here are, of course:

Marrou, H.-I., *Saint Augustin et la fin de la culture antique* (Paris, 1938)

Lorenz, R., 'Die Herkunft des augustinischen Frui Deo', *ZKG* 64 (1952/53) 34–60

Lorenz, R., 'Die Wissenschaftslehre Augustins', *ZKG* 67 (1955/56) 29–60, 213–51

Chapter Five
AUGUSTINE ON MAGIC: A NEGLECTED SEMIOTIC THEORY

Introduction

Historians should take heed of the anthropologist's warning: 'To try to understand magic as an idea in itself, what is the essence of it, as it were, is a hopeless task. It becomes more intelligible when it is viewed not only in relation to empirical activities but also in relation to other beliefs, as part of a system of thought . . .'[1] Especially in the case of magic in Antiquity: for as A. D. Nock once remarked, 'In [the modern] sense it [magic] means the attempt to divert the course of nature by methods which to our science appear to be of a non-rational kind, or which to the user appear to rest on some peculiar wisdom: the charming of warts we call magic, birth-control we do not. We distinguish it from science which proceeds by rational methods, and from religion which if it seems to influence the course of events does so by asking some superior being or beings to do what is needed either by operating directly by some kind of sympathetic action or again compelling the superior being or beings.' But, Nock insisted, this modern use of 'magic' 'does not fit the ancient world. . . There is not, then, as with us, a sphere of magic in contrast to the sphere of religion.'[2]

1 E. P. Evans-Pritchard, *Theories of primitive religion* (Oxford, 1965) 111.

2 A. D. Nock, 'Paul and the magus', *Essays on religion and the ancient world* 1 (Cambridge, Mass., 1972) 308–30, at 313–14. Nock refers (215 n. 32) to F. Pfister's 'admirable article' in *RE* Supp. iv. 323 ff. in this connection. Cf. also his n. 43.

It may be that 'magic' occupied a different place in antiquity on the map of human activities than it does in modern times, especially in relation to ancient science – at least on the comparatively rare occasions when ancient science emerges into clarity from the mists of magic, as, for instance, in the case of Hippocrates[3] – and to ancient religion. Modern anthropological discussions have made such exercises in mapping very hazardous. The sharp distinction that used to be drawn between religion and magic has become increasingly untenable; the two must be located on a continuous scale. The distinction between magic and religion has generally come to be seen not in terms of two different forms of activity, or two different kinds of relation to the supernatural, but rather as the distinction between socially approved and socially disapproved, deviant, forms of ritual behaviour. Magical activity takes place within the framework of a particular religious tradition, and is, so to speak, parasitic upon it, lives within it as its matrix.[4]

I shall be attempting to describe not ancient magic itself, but something much simpler, and also much rarer in antiquity: some of the attempts made by some ancient thinkers to understand the magic current in their own society. It will cause us no surprise that the ancients did not generally consider magic in the manner that sophisticated twentieth century anthropologists would prefer; but we must put up with that.

As a working definition we may start with one given in a recent discussion of early medieval magic: 'Magic may be said

3 *Ibid.*, 317.

4 For a survey of approaches by anthropologists, see M. & R. Wax, 'The notion of magic', *Current anthropology* 4 (1963) 495–518, with the comments and reply in the 'CA treatment', 503–17. For their application to ancient magic, see D. E. Aune, 'Magic in early Christianity', *ANRW* II.23.2 (1980) 1507–57. For more general discussions see: S. J. Tambiah, 'Form and meaning of magical acts: a point of view', in *Modes of thought*, ed. R. Horton & R. Finnegan (London, 1973) 199–229, at 199: '. . .magical acts are ritual acts, and ritual acts are in turn performative acts whose positive

to be the exercise of preternatural control over nature by human beings, with the assistance of forces more powerful than they'.[5] This, while it begs many questions, also has the corresponding virtue of leaving many of those important for us open, and of admitting a large variety of practices under the heading of 'magic'.

The practice of magic was ubiquitous in Antiquity; theorising about it was rare. The only sophisticated attempt at a theory I know of is Augustine's; but to place it in some sort of intellectual context, we must start with teasing out some scraps of theory from other Late Antique writers. It is a meagre harvest; but, broadly, in so far as any 'theory' can be identified, we can discern two main directions of thought. They correspond roughly to two ways many modern interpretations of magic have attempted to explain magical rites. These explanations are open to many objections, but, for all that, these are the lines followed, by and large, by ancient theory.

The first sees magic as dependent on a cosmology of world-harmony, or universal sympathy: you do something here, and as a consequence something happens there. To quote from the beginning of Plotinus's exposition of the subject:

> But how does magic (*goeteia*) work? By sympathy and by the fact that there is a natural concord of things that are alike and opposition of things that are different . . .[6]

---

and creative meaning is missed and whose persuasive validity is misjudged if they are subjected to that kind of empirical verification associated with scientific activity', and pp. 218–27 on their non-scientific, ritual, character. *Id.*, *Magic science, religion and the scope of morality* (The Lewis Henry Morgan Lectures, 1984. Cambridge, 1989) contains a wide-ranging discussion of the concepts and their history in anthropological thought. On their application in the study of Antiquity, see G. E. R. Lloyd, *Magic, reason, experience* (Cambridge, 1979).

5 V. I. J. Flint, *The rise of magic in early medieval Europe* (Oxford, 1991) 3. Cf. my review of the book in *EHR* 107 (1992) 378–80.

6 Plotinus, *Enn.* IV.4.40 (trans. A. H. Armstrong). The discussion extends to 4.44.

To leave it at this is, no doubt, to oversimplify the thought of one of the greatest thinkers of Late Antiquity; but it will do for our present purpose, which is to point to a general direction, not to give an account of his subtle and complex cosmology. The efficacy of magical rituals depends, on such a view, on natural forces. The laws governing these connections may be unknown to most of us, may be hidden even from the magician; but it is in virtue of organic, natural, relationships, the rational harmony built into the cosmos – the *carmen uniuersitatis* as Augustine would call it[7] – that magic works. Ancients were no less ready than we are to discriminate between genuine and charlatan claims to the expertise which enables the nexus of things to be exploited by various techniques. Magic is in effect a branch of physics. In our modern terms such a theory would translate into a theory of magic as false science.[8]

The second view considered magic as dependent on collaboration with demons: forming a community with them, so that whatever happens is a consequence of demonic power brought to the aid of the magician. Religion and magic belong together as against 'scientific' manipulations of phenomena. They are distinguished on other grounds: most fundamentally according to whether they are generally approved (for whatever reasons) or disapproved. We might, for convenience, designate this distinction a 'sociological' one. Just how magic is related to religion in this view is a question that will receive different answers according to what the religion concerned is. Generally we can perceive a strong tendency to treat magic as a parody or perversion of true religion. This second notion seems to have been the more commonly held, though it is often found in combination with the first.

These two ways of thinking of magical activity did not

---

7 *De musica* VI.11.29.

8 For a widely known example of treating magic among medical (and pseudo-medical) 'remedies', see Pliny *HN* XXXVIII and XXX.1.

generally have to be distinguished in Antiquity, and it was easy to hold them side by side. There was no pressure on non-Christians to distinguish the exercise of a scientific *techne* from recourse to the help of higher powers; both were quite legitimate activities. But in a Christian perspective this ambiguity had to be banished; for if a magical rite was not a case of exercising the art of medicine, or some other natural *techne*, then it must be a religious, though false, and therefore blasphemous, ritual. If magic is demonic and the demonic is wicked, idolatrous or godless, then there is a new and urgent need to distinguish between scientific activity and religious ritual. (Origen may stand for Christian thinkers in general in drawing so sharp a contrast between magic and true religion, leaving a separate, neutral, area to be occupied by human techniques based on the natural sciences.[9]) The sharp distinction between magic and science is a result of Christian pressure on a range of activities which could often remain undifferentiated. In a Christian perspective, if a rite was neither the exercise of a human *ars*, nor the performance of an approved rite of Christian worship, then it was necessarily demonic magic. Augustine's views on astrology (closely related to those on magic and divination) provide a good example of this manner of driving a wedge between what we might describe as 'scientific' and as 'superstitious' predictions.[10] As *artes*, that of the *mathematicus* and that of *diuinatio* were now radically distinguished, even though the terminology remained fluid.

Christians shared with almost all their contemporaries in Antiquity a sense of living in a world surrounded by invisible

9 In *C. Cels*. VIII.61 Origen commends the medical arts and prayer to God for healing bodily infirmity as better than the ministrations of demons. Christian thinkers were not always equally clear on this subject.

10 Cf. the fine study by B. Bruning, 'De l'astrologie à la grâce', in *Collectanea Augustiniana: Mélanges T. J. Van Bavel*, t. 2 (Roma, 1991) 575–643. Augustine's fullest discussion of the distinction is in *De doctr. Christ.* II.20.30–21.32. Cf. also *De diu. daem.* 1.2, 6.10; *De ciu. Dei* V.9.

powers.[11] These powers could be benevolent or malevolent; the important point for us is that they were *there*. For Plato they were intermediaries between men and the gods (e.g. *Sympos.* 202E–203A; for comment, see Augustine *De ciuitate Dei* VIII. 18). In Christian eyes the gods, and any power that allowed men to communicate with them, were sinister powers of evil. The *daimon* and the gods were subsumed within the class of demons; and they became 'demonic'. It is in this perspective they saw all pagan magical, divinatory, and similar rites. Thus Firmicus Maternus, for instance, caricatured the non-Christian rites of the fourth century as counterfeits of the true Christian rites.[12] Conversely, the pagan Celsus was very ready to believe that Christians got their powers from the demons.[13] Origen, in his reply to Celsus, consistently attributes the power of magical rites to demons, and contrasts their wickedness with the goodness of God.[14]

Augustine's 'theory' of magic

Augustine's theory of magic is cast, as one would expect, within the context of the cosmology he shared with Late Antique people at large. The structure of his spiritual universe was, in effect, not very different from, to take a particularly fine example, Porphyry's.[15] Porphyry's world contains good and bad demons within a monotheistic universe (II.37; 103–

11 N. Brox, 'Magie und Aberglaube an den Anfängen des Christentums', *Trierer theol. Zeits.* 83 (1974) 157–80 contains a useful survey; 172–79 on Augustine.

12 Cf. *De errore prof. rel.* 18–27.

13 *Apud* Origen, *C. Cels.* I.6.

14 See especially *C. Cels.* I.60; II.51; VII.69; VIII.36 (on angels and demons); 59–60. Cf. Lactantius, *Diu. Inst.* II.15–17.

15 Porphyre, *De l'abstinence*, ed. & trad. J. Bouffartigue & M. Patillon (Paris, 1977–79). References in this paragraph (in brackets) are given to this edition, Book II, chapter and page number in vol. 2. I wish to thank Hilary Armstrong for drawing my attention to this text.

04); the good demons rule over both natural processes and human souls and their activities when engaged in their proper *technai*, notably the liberal arts, education, music, gymnastics, medicine (II.38.2; 104). The bad demons delude, master and collude with wicked, turbulent and rebellious human beings (II.40; 106–07). They hate and seek to harm the human race. Good demons communicate with the human race through significant action (*semainomena*) such as dreams, inspired words or other means; bad ones through sorcery (*goeteia*) (II.41; 108). This cosmology and its attendant concept of magic has very close affinities with Augustine's.

Some of the fundamental ideas that came to dominate Augustine's views on magic appear in his earliest formal discussion of this subject in the context of a question about the efficacy of magical rites performed by Pharaoh's magicians and the way they differ from the wonders performed by 'God's servants'. A somewhat muddled discussion begins with a distinction which seems oddly remote, but is in fact crucial to all his reflection on this theme: the 'private' and the 'public' laws which govern individual action. The spirits which govern every agent in the visible world do so in accordance with both private and public law; piety subjects the private to the public, obeying the latter willingly, for 'the universal law is divine wisdom.' The more any agent turns aside from God to his private good, the more he is turned in upon himself and subjected to 'those powers which desire their own private good, to be honoured by men like gods'. To these powers divine law often concedes, through a private law (*priuato illo iure*: perhaps translate 'that [i.e. the public, divine, law] being negated'), the ability to assist those who are subjected to them with a certain power akin to the miraculous (*miraculorum aliquid*); but where divine law rules as a public law, it overcomes private licence. Magicians, thus, work private quasi-miracles for selfish ends; whereas visible 'miracles' are wrought by God's servants when it is deemed – by God, presumably – useful for them to have this power; and it is wielded in accordance with that 'public and imperial law' which governs the universe, 'that is to say, they command the lower powers according to God's supreme power . . . In them God Himself commands, for they are His temples, and they burn with love of Him, despising their own private power.'[16] The opposition between 'public' and 'private', a doublet which was to remain fundamental in much of Augustine's thought,[17] is the key to the distinction between magicians' wonders and miracles of the saints: the former mobilise the powers they control (through secret pacts, Augustine suspects) for their own, selfish and partial ends; the latter mobilise powers subject to God for disinterested, 'public', ends, in line with God's universal purposes.

So the things done by magicians and by saints are often alike; but in fact they are done 'for different ends and by different rights' (*diuerso fine et diuerso iure*): 'for the magicians do them seeking their own glory, the saints seeking God's glory; the former carry them out . . . as private

---

16 *De diu. quaest. LXXXIII* 79.1. The work consists of notes taken on discussions held by Augustine with his *fratres* prior to his episcopal ordination, collected into a book – *Retract.* I.26. I see no good grounds for denying the authenticity of this question. For a later treatment of this theme, see *De Trin.* III.7.12.

17 On the fundamental opposition in Augustine's mind between *commune* and *priuatum*, the key text is *Enarr. in Ps.* 103.ii.11. Lying here emerges as the archetypal 'private' utterance. See also: *De Trin.* X.5.7; XII.9.14; *De Gen. c. Man.* II.16.24; *Ep.* 140.26.63; *De cons. euang.* I.19.24. The relevance of the concept to Augustine's views on astrology has been noted by Bruning (*art. cit.*, above, n. 10) 620. The centrality of the notion of the 'private' to much of Augustine's thought still needs a thorough study. See, however, my remarks in *Saeculum. History and society in the theology of Saint Augustine*, 2nd ed. (Cambridge, 1988) xvii–xviii and 60; and in *The end of ancient Christianity* (Cambridge, 1990) 77–79. See also my '*De ciuitate dei*: Pride and the common good', *Proceedings of the PMR Conference*, 12–13 (1989) 1–16; also in: *Collectanea Augustiniana: Augustine: 'Second Founder of the Faith'*, ed. J. C. Schnabelt & F. van Fleteren (New York &c., 1990) 245–59.

transactions or sorceries (*quasi priuata commercia uel uenefi-cia*); the latter as public ministry (*publica administratione*) in obedience to Him to whom all creatures are subject . . . Hence it is one thing when magicians perform wonders, another when good Christians . . . perform them: magicians do it through private contracts [with the evil powers], good Christians through public righteousness . . .'[18] This 'socio-logical' way of contrasting magic and religion in terms of their 'private' or 'public' character, with reference to a moral community, has distinctly Durkheimian overtones.[19] It is, moreover, very much in line with the criteria invoked by Late Roman writers and legislators to distinguish magic from religion.[20]

The essential ground for the distinction between miracles worked by saints and those worked by magicians seems to be the end for which they are respectively performed, God's glory and the public good, *versus* their own, selfish and private ends. There appears to be a subordinate distinction between the powers respectively invoked by magicians and saints: the former's accomplices obey them in virtue of a prior

18 *De diu. quaest. LXXXIII* 79.4 (reading *ueneficia*, not, with some MSS, *beneficia*).

19 See E. Durkheim, *Elementary forms of the religious life* (New York, 1965) 57–63, who refers (n. 62) to Robertson Smith in this connection; and on Durkheim, see Aune, 'Magic in early Christianity' (above, n. 4) at 1514–15. Aune here suggests that 'The sociological description of the nature and function of magic in relation to religion . . . appears to be the most satisfying theoretical perspective from which to analyze magic in Graeco-Roman religions', and gives references (n. 27) to 'some significant studies of social deviance'. J. Goody, 'Religion and ritual: the definitional problem', *Br. J. of Sociol.* 12 (1961) 142–64, who criticises (145) Durkheim's 'sacred/profane' dichotomy as not universally applicable. Cf. M. Douglas, *Purity and danger* (London, 1966) 22, 58–72.

20 See Nock, *op. cit.* (above, n. 2) 315–18. 'What gets the name of magic is a varied complex of things, mainly *qua* professional or *qua* criminal in intent or *qua* alien' (317–18). Nock refers (316) as an important illustration to Constantine's law, *C.Th.* IX.16.3.

pact of association; the latter invoke divine power or its agencies. Though of crucial importance to Christian preachers,[21] for our purpose this difference may be ignored, for both give magic a semiotic explanation: it is the result of communication and shared meanings. In neither case is the efficacy of the act direct, mobilising a natural force, like manipulating a mechanism, pulling a lever; rather, it is mediated by spiritual beings, involving wills and intelligence. Augustine's explanation of magical (including miraculous) efficacy follows in the track of the second of the ancient traditions distinguished above (see p. 128) – the explanation in terms of mobilising demonic powers rather than in terms of cosmic 'sympathy'. Religion, in the words of a recent study, is 'magic made respectable';[22] magic belongs, phenomenologically, to the same realm of action as sacraments.[23] Both, for Augustine, were systems of communication: for 'human beings cannot share a religion, whether true or false, without being associated within it by means of some shared system of symbols or visible rituals [*nisi aliquo signaculorum vel sacramentorum visibilium consortio colligentur*]'.[24] His account of magic would allow us easily to understand the more or less permanent state of competition between what in any particular society is recognised as 'religion' and as 'magic'.

His fullest discussion, in the *De doctrina Christiana*, is entirely in line with this. The work was the outcome of Augustine's preoccupation with the problems of learning, teaching, and, at the most fundamental level, of communication. This preoccupation set the context for his fullest and richest account of magic. Here the germs of the explanation

21 For instance to John Chrysostom: see A. A. Barb, 'The survival of the magic arts', in *The Conflict between paganism and Christianity in the fourth century*, ed. A. Momigliano (Oxford, 1963) 100–25, at 106.

22 Flint (see above, n. 5), 32.

23 See the remarks of Mary Douglas, *Natural symbols* (London, 1970) 8, and below, p. 145.

24 See below, n. 27.

given in the early work are filled out within the framework of a fully fledged theory of signs.[25] Augustine devotes several chapters (II.20.30–24.37) to idolatrous, magical, divinatory, or astrological practices which he groups together under the heading of 'superstitions'. The class comprises practices (*quicquid institutum est ab hominibus*) that pertain to the making and worshipping of idols, or to the worship of creatures, or parts of creatures, as divine; also 'consultations and pacts about certain meanings agreed with demons by contract, such as the undertakings (*molimina*) of the magical arts'. Haruspication, augury, amulets and charms 'also condemned by medical science', ligatures and 'thousands of vacuous observances', Augustine tells us, all belong here (II.20.30–31).

Book II of this work explores the question of how communities are constituted by the way they understand and use the symbolic systems (i.e. all that Augustine includes under his category of *signa data*) established within them. Any human group is defined by the boundaries of the system of signs in use among its members. On Augustine's theory signs mean something to somebody; the somebodies who agree on their meaning constitute a (linguistic) community. In the *De doctrina Christiana* Augustine makes use of his general semiological theory to explore the relationships of groups sharing a culture, or of sub-cultures within a society.

Superstitious practices link demons and human beings into an association created by a 'pact' or an 'agreement'. Magical and other 'superstitious' practices rest on 'pacts about certain meanings agreed with demons by contract (*pacta quaedam significationum cum daemonibus placita atque foederata*)' (II.20.30). The idea of such agreements is at first sight puzzling: magicians and soothsayers do not obviously make agreements with demons and then go on to use the con-

25 On this see my paper 'Signs, communication and communities in Augustine's *De doctrina Christiana*' (Chapter 4 above) where, however, I did not consider magic fully.

ventions agreed on. But Augustine insists on this 'pact' repeatedly, in language of almost legal precision.[26] He leaves us in no doubt that he thought of the agreed symbolic system as the bond of association: 'these arts of idle and noxious superstition [are] constituted by a certain association through faithless and deceitful friendship (*pacta infidelis et dolosae amicitiae*)' (II.23.36); 'they [omens, auguries etc.] are valid only to the extent that they have been established by presumptuous minds as a common language agreed with demons (*tantum ualent, quantum praesumptione animorum quasi communi quadam lingua cum daemonibus foederata sunt*)' (II.24.37). Like words,

> all these meanings are understood according to the conventions of the society, and, as these conventions differ, are understood differently; nor are they agreed upon among men because they already had a meaning, but they receive their meaning from the agreement' (*hae omnes significationes pro suae cuiusque societatis consensione animos mouent et, quia diuersa consensio est, diuerse mouent, nec ideo consenserunt in eas homines, quia iam ualebant ad significationem, sed ideo ualent quia consenserunt in eas – II.24.37*).

Leaving aside, for the moment, the puzzle about the status and origin of this pact of association between men and demons, what Augustine's account makes wholly clear is that magic and the like are symbolic systems, a language of words, signs and rituals, which, in the first place, secure the association of men and demons; and, in doing so, establish the cohesion of the group on which the magical efficacy of its rites rests. 'Men cannot be brought together', Augustine wrote

---

26 *De doctr. Christ.* II.20.30; 22.34; 23.36; 24.37; 25.38; 39.58. The same notion is adumbrated in *De diu. quaest. LXXXIII* 79.1 (cf. above, p. 132), and used regularly by Augustine, e.g. in *Sermo Dolbeau* 6.11, *REAug* 39 (1993) 97–106, 103.

soon after working out his views on symbolic communities in the *De doctrina Christiana*, 'in the name of any religion, whether true or false, without being associated by means of some shared visible symbols or rituals'.[27]

Turning, now, to the puzzling 'pact' by which wicked men associate with demons, it is not immediately clear how Augustine wishes us to construe this. It was clear to Augustine that if the meanings of expressions are 'conventional' in the sense that their links with their referents are not fixed by nature, they are, nevertheless, not freely chosen by the language-user, but imposed by the conventions of the existing linguistic community, its habits and traditions.[28] You do not *choose* to use the language of demons, thereby entering a community with them; rather, you belong to their community, so you speak their language. The primary fact is the belonging; by belonging, one comes to share the language that constitutes this community of human and demonic beings. A clue to how he is thinking of the establishment of such conventions can be found in his earlier discussion of magic (see above, p. 132) in *De diu. quaest. LXXXIII* 79.1. There Augustine envisages a community brought into being through evil men, seeking their own, selfish and 'private' ends, being assisted by demonic powers similarly intent on their own, 'private', glorification. The community sharing a symbolic system is brought into being by the identity of intentions. It must be the intention to enter such an association that lies at the roots of the conventions which hold it together. It is as if a

27 *In nullum autem nomen religionis, seu uerum seu falsum, coagulari homines possunt, nisi aliquo signaculorum uel sacramentorum uisibilium consortio colligentur* (C. *Faust.* XIX.11).

28 Cf. Augustine, *Conf.* I.18.29: *Vide, domine Deus, et patienter, ut vides, vide quomodo diligenter observent filii hominum pacta litterarum et syllabarum accepta a prioribus locutoribus. . .*; cf. F. de Saussure, *Cours de linguistique générale*, publiée par C. Bally, A. Sechehaye & A. Riedlinger, 3rd. ed. (Paris, 1967): 'Si par rapport à l'idée qu'il représente, le signifiant apparaît comme librement choisi, en revanche, par rapport à la communauté linguistique qui l'emploie, il n'est pas libre, il est imposé' (p. 104).

person entered the 'contract' with the demons in the very movement of his will towards the demons with whom he associates himself.

There is much in the *De doctrina Christiana* to confirm this crucial role assigned to intention. Intention, for instance, is decisive in determining the meaning to be given to certain polysemic symbols. Augustine notes that there are practices which can be ambiguous: hanging certain objects on one's body, for instance, or taking certain foods or drinks, might be either sinister acts of superstition, or sensible medication (II.20.30; cf. 29.45). Augustine seems to treat such signs as capable of belonging to two different sign systems: either to a language resting on demonic convention, or to something different, resting, harmlessly, on human contrivance. Which of the two symbol systems the particular rite belongs to is determined by the agent's intention. Augustine's explanation differs from, for instance, Porphyry's (see above, pp. 130–31) mainly by assigning the initiative in magical transactions to the human rather than the demonic partners.

Crucial for Augustine's view of magic is this anchorage of sign systems in intentionality. Meaning is bound up with will. This colours all he has to say about them in the *De doctrina Christiana*.[29] From the start of the work the will is central: 'We are on a road, one which is a road not from place to place, but a road of the affections' (I.17.16; cf. I.36.41). So communication between sentient beings involves more than the

29 See on this the contributions to the Notre Dame symposium *De doctrina Christiana: A classic of Western culture*, ed. D. W. H. Arnold & P. Bright (Christianity and Judaism in Antiquity, vol. 9. University of Notre Dame Press, 1995) by W. S. Babcock, '*Caritas* and signification in *De doctrina christiana* 1–3', and by D. Dawson, 'Sign theory, allegory and the motions of the soul in the *De doctrina christiana*', to both of which I owe much. See also M. D. Jordan, 'Words and word: Incarnation and signification in Augustine's *De doctrina christiana*', *AugSt* 11 (1980) 177–96: '. . .an intentional sign is the kind of thing which starts a motion towards what it signifies and, mediately, towards whomever employs it as a sign' (186).

manipulation of disembodied signs: hearing a voice 'we attend to the motion of the mind' (*affectionem animi* – II.1.1); speech requires us to respond to the speaker's inner disposition, and, similarly, communicating with others by signs we seek to 'make another a participant of our will' (*uoluntatis nostrae participem* – II.3.4). The speech-act performed overtly in any act of communication 'brings forth', or 'expresses', an inner movement of the mind (*quod animo gerimus*; . . . *gerit*; . . . *quod corde gestamus*; I.13.12; II.2.3; I.13.12).[30] It seems that it is this affective element, the presence of will within acts of communication, that Augustine's 'pact' with demonic powers ultimately rests on. Some speech-acts, he seems to be saying, are demonic from their inception in virtue of the direction of the speaker's 'affections'. Their significance unfolds within a community created by the selfish, 'private', purposes. The superstitious rites of magic and similar 'demonic' observances thus pertain 'to a [system of signs] not divinely instituted for the sake of the love of God and the neighbour, as it were publicly, but they dissipate the hearts of the wretched through the private desire of temporal things' (II.23.36). This society of men and demons being 'constituted, as it were, by a pact of faithless and deceitful friendship' (see above, p. 132), is self-stultifying in that the pattern of signification is constantly subverted within it by the 'spirits who wish to deceive', manipulating the signs 'so that they affect different people in different ways, according to their own thoughts and presumptions (*ideo diuersis diuerse proueniunt secundum cogitationes et praesumptiones suas*)' (*ibid.*). 'Far from joining person to person in genuine sociality, then, such a world-view actually caters to their private desires, reinforces their separate presumptions, and thus tacitly undermines the very social order that it appears to secure.'[31] Magic is the language of a group which parodies and undermines a true social order.

30 This has been well brought out by Dawson (see above, n. 29).
31 Babcock (see above, n. 29).

On the lines of Augustine's exposition we should not, then, interpret magic as failed science, or pseudo-science; it belongs, rather, to the realm of illocutionary or performative acts such as we have in ritual: '. . . magical acts are ritual acts, and ritual acts are in turn performative acts whose positive and creative meaning is missed and whose persuasive validity is misjudged if they are subjected to that kind of empirical verification associated with scientific activity'.[32] It might be pressing anachronism too far to suggest that the illocutionary force of a magical rite is entry into a demonic society, its perlocutionary aim the performance or occurrence of certain acts, events, or states of affairs; that, to use J. L. Austin's language, *in* performing a magical rite or uttering an incantation one is entering into such a relationship, and that *by* doing so one intends to bring about something.[33] But something like this would be in line with Augustine's view.

Magic and cognate rites

In a study[34] of the efficacy of a Jewish ritual Jacob Milgrom concludes that for Judaism 'it was inconceivable that any rite was inherently efficacious. In the absence of rational explanation there was, solely and sufficiently, the inscrutable will of

32 S. J. Tambiah, 'Form and meaning of magical acts: a point of view', in *Modes of thought*, ed. R. Horton & R. Finnegan (see above, n. 4) 199–229, at 199.

33 Cf. M. Hancher, 'Performative utterance, the Word of God, and the death of the author', *Semeia* 41 (1988) (*Speech act theory and biblical criticism*, ed. H. C. White) 27–40. I owe knowledge of this to the kindness of John Gager.

34 'The paradox of the Red Cow', in *Studies in cultic theology and terminology* (Studies in Judaism in Late Antiquity, 36. Leiden, 1983) 85–93. Quotation from p. 93. See also his 'Magic, monotheism and the sin of Moses', in *The Quest for the Kingdom of God: Studies in honor of E. Mendenhall*, ed. H. B. Huffmon, F. A. Spina & A. R. W. Green (Winona Lake, Indiana, 1983) 251–65. I wish to thank Mary Douglas for bringing these marvellous studies to my attention, as well as for much other generous advice.

God.' The efficacy of the rite rests simply on God's communication with man and man's with God. God can listen to the
prayer of his faithful, and He can promise to come to their aid;
but He cannot be coerced by human words or acts. His
sovereign freedom and monopoly of power is what distinguishes the miracles wrought by Moses and Aaron from the
wonders worked by pagan magicians. Milgrom has traced
with great elegance the emergence of Jewish monotheism from
its pagan milieu, and characterised in a wonderfully persuasive
manner that which distinguishes the one from the other. This
can help us to understand Augustine's way of making sense of
magic, for it is cast in a similar mould: like Milgrom's
monotheistic Jew, Augustine refuses to credit any human
ritual act with intrinsic power.

Augustine's theory of magic (if we may, as we surely may,
call it a 'theory') remained remarkably constant throughout his
career. From the early discussions with his *fratres* (see above,
n. 16) to the polemic in the *City of God* VIII–X his view
remains, in substance, unchanged. The only major development it seems to have undergone in the course of his career is its
incorporation in a wider theory of signs, communication, and
community in the *De doctrina Christiana*.[35] This was not
devised to provide a framework within which an explanation
of magic could be articulated; but once formulated, it was a
powerful theory with wide bearings in a number of disparate
areas, and it lurks in the background of Augustine's treatment
of a number of themes, including magic.[36] Prayer, sacraments,

35 Also hinted at in the roughly contemporary *De fide et symbolo*,
preached at the Council of Carthage, 393.

36 See the studies of C. P. Mayer, especially *Die Zeichen in der geistigen
Entwicklung und in der Theologie des jungen Augustinus* (Cassiciacum, 24/
1. Würzburg, 1969); and *Die Zeichen in der geistigen Entwicklung und in
der Theologie Augustinus*: II. Teil: *Die antimanichäische Epoche* (Cassiciacum, 24/2. Würzburg, 1974). For a bibliography, see my paper referred to
above, n. 25 [= Chapter 4 here]. The theory clearly underlies the *De
diuinatione daemonum*.

exorcism, the cult of relics, as well as magical rites, are among the practices on which Augustine's notion of signs might be expected to shed light. He accounts for magic and sacramental ritual in what are essentially the same, semiotic, terms. Both are systems of signs, in use in rival speech communities. One set of signs has validity in a perverse community of individuals working for their own selfish ends and deceiving each other, the other in a community united in their service of God and of the common good.

Augustine's theology of the *ex opere operato* efficacy of sacraments, especially of baptism, even if administered by schismatic or unworthy ministers, has often been held to have encouraged a magical view of sacramental efficacy.[37] It is important, however, to be clear that such *ex opere operato* efficacy did not involve, for Augustine, the direct efficacy of word or rite at the cost of the elision of spiritual (in this case divine) agency. Writing of the eucharist, in one of his most summary passages Augustine observed that 'so far as the action of human hands is concerned . . . it is not consecrated to be so great a sacrament (*sacramentum*: 'mystery'?) except by the invisible working of God's Spirit . . .' (*De Trin.* III.4.10). The alleged 'magicisation' of the rite is usually held to appear in the fact that the communal dimension of the rite and the element of intentionality in it were by-passed, and its efficacy construed as a direct mechanical transaction, without the mediation of any spiritual agency. The spell came to take

---

37 For instance, A. Angenendt, 'Taufe und Politik im frühen Mittelalter', *Frühmittelalterliche Studien* 7 (1973) 143–68, at 147 observes that Augustine's views on the efficacy of baptism 'scheint nie vergessen. . .'. For a remarkable study of baptismal theology in terms of the kinds of social context which encourage – or discourage – certain conceptions of ritual efficacy, see J. Patout Burns, 'On Rebaptism: Social Organization in the Third Century', *Journal of early Christian studies* 1 (1993) 367–403. For a somewhat unsatisfactory attempt to exonerate Augustine, see E. G. Weltin, 'The concept of *ex opere operato* efficacy in the Fathers as an evidence of magic in early Christianity', *GRBS* 3 (1960) 74–100.

the place of prayer and invocation.[38] Meaning has ceased to be, so it is said, something to be understood within a speech-community.

Moreover, this model of magical efficacy is thought to have encouraged wider ripples of imagined or expected control over events: baptism, for instance, came to be expected to bring political (and other) success, bodily as well as spiritual health, and so forth.[39] It was, so it is generally held, only a short step from an *ex opere operato* theology of the sacraments to a wider magical interpretation of ritual action; and the Reformation, on such a view, will tend to appear as a deliverance from a mechanical ritualism, even from 'magic'.[40] This is too vast a theme to discuss here; moreover, Augustine's theology of baptism cuts confusingly across the grain of some of his reflection on ritual action. I therefore consider another, and less well known theme as an example.

A revealing case is furnished by the cult of the dead at the tomb, and especially the custom of burial near the tomb of a saint ('*ad sanctos*'), a question Augustine considered with particular care, in his response to that devoted promoter of the cult, Paulinus of Nola. We have been given a careful study of Augustine's view and of contemporary practice as revealed in funerary inscriptions by Mme Yvette Duval.[41] Her conclusions will save us the task of surveying the evidence and

38 The two often overlap, as S. J. Tambiah observes in 'The magical power of words', *Man* n.s. 3 (1968) 175–208.

39 See Angenendt, n. 37, above.

40 Cf. Douglas, in *Natural symbols* (see above, n. 23) 10, 47ff. Also, for some of the debate over K. Thomas, *Religion and the decline of magic* (London, 1971) see H. Geertz, 'An anthropology of religion and magic, I', *J. of Interdisciplinary History* 6 (1975) 71–89 and K. Thomas, 'An anthropology of religion and magic, II', *J. of Interdisciplinary History* 6 (1975) 91–109 (reply to Geertz). On Reformation views , see B. Vogler, 'La Réforme et le concept de miracle au XVIe siècle', *Revue d'histoire de la spiritualité* 48 (1972) 145–50.

41 *Auprès des saints corps et âme. L'inhumation «ad sanctos» dans la chrétienté d'Orient et d'Occident du IIIe au VIIe siècle* (Paris, 1988).

analysing Augustine's text. Augustine's answer to Paulinus is stark and simple: the dead cannot expect any benefit from the *place* of their burial, only from the prayers of the living who may visit the place. Place by itself has no efficacy: 'what may benefit the spirit of the dead is not the place of its dead body but the living affection of a mother kindled by the memory attached to the place (*ex loci memoria uiuus matris affectus*)' (*De cura pro mort. ger.* 6). This belief is frequently attested by funerary inscriptions (and, incidentally, by Gregory the Great, *Dial.* IV.52) which express the hope that the dead might be received among the elect thanks to the prayers of his friends and relatives (as well as his merits). Such an understanding of these burial practices accords well with the thought of Augustine, Gregory, and other reflective thinkers and churchmen. But, as Mme Duval has shown, there is also another current of thought to be found among these inscriptions: that the dead body keeps a trace of the spirit it had lived by, which operates through the bodily remains on those in contact with or proximity to it.[42] There is a wide gap between popular belief in the direct magical efficacy of the buried saint's remains and Augustine's determination not to short-circuit prayer and God's providence.

What are we to make of this difference in views, on the one hand as represented by Augustine, on the other, by the many epitaphs, hagiographical stories and images which attest another, and perhaps more widespread notion?

We are apt, as I have said, to think this way of short-circuiting the symbolic element of ritual action as turning the action into a pseudo-scientific act, and then to interpret such an act – presumably because there is a widely diffused notion among us of magic as 'pseudo-scientific' – as 'magical', in contradistinction to 'religious'. Augustine would certainly not have interpreted it in this way. He would not have seen 'magic' at work, because the essential element of communication with

42 Duval, *op. cit.*, 211.

the demonic world was absent. On the other hand, he might well have admitted that it fell short of the properly 'religious', for it by-passed the element of communication with the divine. He seems, rather, to have taken it upon himself, in his treatise on *The care for the dead*, to supply this suppressed element. He appears to have thought that what was lacking in popular piety was the explicit articulation of something which was, nevertheless, present.

The short-circuiting of prayer in the rite could perhaps be understood in terms of Mary Douglas's discussion of 'ritual-ism'. This attitude she defines as 'sensitivity to condensed symbols';[43] a sensitivity which will be operative in both sacramental and magical behaviour.

> The Bog Irishman in his faithfulness to the rule of Friday abstinence is undeniably like the primitive ritualist. Magi-cal rules have always an expressive function. Whatever other functions they perform, disciplinary, anxiety-reducing, or sanctioning of moral codes, they have first and foremost a symbolic function. The official symbol-ism of Friday abstinence was originally personal mortifi-cation, a small weekly celebration of Good Friday. Thus it pointed directly to Calvary and Redemption.[44]

Could we say that burying our dead near the holy burials is a similar piece of ritualism? Acting as a condensed symbol of the communion of saints, enacted whenever one of the living prays at the graveside, and tenaciously adhered to even when the original symbolism is forgotten – just as Friday abstinence continued to be? If we accept this, then the modern (and discredited) idea that 'magic' tends to be 'manipulative' whereas 'religion' is 'supplicative' is beside the mark. Popular

43 *Natural symbols* (above, n. 23) 8.
44 *Ibid.*, 37. For parallel 'learned' interpretations of the healing action of relics, see A. Rousselle, *Croire et guérir: La foi en Gaule dans l'Antiquité tardive* (Paris, 1990) 231–50.

piety has condensed prayer and ritual into a single act, not fully explicated. Augustine has simply supplied the missing explication.

To sum up: Augustine distinguishes two semiotic structures. One is authentically public, shared by the whole language-using community, and is used by its members to communicate with one another as well as with God; the other is a 'private' code, restricted to some members of this community and used only by them, to communicate with demons. Magic is part of this second semiotic system.[45]

---

45 Cf. Bruning (see above, n. 10) 614: 'On pourrait dire qu'[Augustin] aborde la *superstitio* comme un phénomène linguistique'.